DYE
YOUR
HAIR
PURPLE
SOONER

5 Steps to Becoming the Legendary Leader
of Your Technicolour Life

(Purple hair optional!)

LORRAINE HAMILTON

ISBN: 9780473556204 (Softcover)
ISBN: 9780473556211 (Ebook)

Other books by Lorraine Hamilton:

Thin[k] Program: The Smart Women's Guide To Effortless Weightloss:
ISBN 9780473227418

Activate Your Life (Contributing Author):
ISBN: 9781700333919

Printed in the United States of America.

Cover Design by 100Covers.com
Interior Design by FormattedBooks.com

This book is dedicated to those who have contributed to my discomfort and helped me to learn, and to those who are willing to choose discomfort in order to live their Technicolour Life.

CONTENTS

PROLOGUE

Before I worked in personal and professional development, I designed mobile phone networks. In job terms, that means I was a radio frequency engineer. The radio frequency spectrum is where all radio waves lie. There is one part of the spectrum—which ranges from really low frequency waves like old school AM radio, right through to gamma rays which are used in radiation therapy—where you can actually *see* the waves. Somewhere near the middle of the spectrum sits natural light. In this tiny, perfectly tuned spot, every single colour of the rainbow lives. And if you tune your life just right—*just as you would tune the radio*—it becomes an explosion of colour and experience.

That is what this book is all about.

It's not about changing who you are. It's about tuning yourself to your perfect channel so that you can be bold, authentic, genuine and happy.

Since 2006, I have been a coach. Over that time, I have worked with countless clients from many different backgrounds and environments working on all aspects of their life, career and business. While there has been diversity in my client base, there have been similarities in the people I have coached; namely, that they are willing to take personal responsibility for their situation, are ambitious, have achieved things in the past, and they are willing to learn and look inside to find the answers and achieve external results.

While there are a multitude of issues that people are dealing with, I discovered that they were all underpinned by a small number of root causes.

The problem is that we don't tend to talk about the challenges that are troubling us. The vast majority of my clients felt that they weren't good enough in some aspect of their life, business or career. When you don't feel good enough in a situation, it is common to not want to draw attention to whatever you believe is lacking and so you keep it to yourself.

However, these feelings are like mushrooms. They need darkness and sh*t to grow! When you keep the feeling of not being good enough to yourself, you are keeping it in the dark, your inner critic voice keeps feeding it nonsense, and the feeling grows.

It's natural to think that you are the only person experiencing something if you never share that feeling with anyone. Yet with every experience brought into the light and shared, the strength of those not-good-enough feelings begins to diminish. This is why it is so important to normalise our experiences and why group therapies and communities are so powerful.

As part of a team that delivers group retreats, I have seen first-hand the power of normalising experiences so that we can succeed collectively. Recently, I began an in-person group of local clients. In this context, I witnessed once again the power of normalising experiences so that we can grow individually and together. Group coaching brings together like-minded people from all across the world to redefine success, set goals that actually work, break through blocks and support each other as they progress towards the life they always wanted to live.

A few definitions...

Legendary Leadership is the umbrella that I use to encapsulate all of this. Legendary Leadership means choosing the temporary discomfort of change over the permanent discomfort of staying where you are. Legendary Leadership is about making bold decisions and being authentic and genuine while you are doing it. And it's not just for leaders of corporations. It's for everyone. And it's especially for you.

You are about to learn how to become the Legendary Leader of your own Technicolour Life, but what does that mean?

Living in glorious technicolour means living 100% as yourself. It means operating in a way that is completely aligned to what's most important to you. It means feeling good in your own skin. It means taking responsibility and action towards the changes you want to see in your life. It means not apologising for who you are. It means taking up space in the world.

Living a Technicolour Life feels like you really *have* got this, even when things are hard. It feels like being brave. It feels like shedding those masks that you might have been wearing. It feels like not having to think about all the characters that you play on a weekly basis. The 'work' you. The 'friend' you. The 'parent' you. The 'daughter' you. The 'partner' you. It feels like being you all the time, in all of those different scenarios. And that feels lighter, freer, and more honest.

When you embrace all of you, you get to live all the colours of the rainbow, not leaving out any facets of yourself. Rather than only being boring old red or plain old blue, you get to spend time in all the subtle shades of purple and pink and orange. It becomes more nuanced, more vibrant, more varied, less autopilot, less humdrum, less hidden, and, well... less grey!

It is knowing yourself so well that decision-making becomes easy. It is forgiving yourself for mistakes so that you can continue to move forward and grow and develop. It is turning up the volume and brightness on all the great things in your life and not apologising for who you are, either inwardly or outwardly, anymore. It is redefining success on your terms, not what others deem success for you. It is about setting your own goals, your own milestones, and your own path. It is taking this one life and designing it to be the one you are most excited about.

Then living it.

How does living a Technicolour Life fit in with the concept of Legendary Leadership?

Legendary Leaders are magnetic. They don't have to be corporate leaders or politicians. Legendary Leaders are everywhere. They are the people who inspire, who motivate, who light the way for others. In order to do that, they need to be bold, authentic and genuine, and that comes from living a Technicolour Life.

> **Bold:**
> *1. (of a person, action, or idea) Showing a willingness to take risks; confident and courageous.*
> *2. (of a colour, design, or shape) Having a strong, vivid, or clear appearance.*

> **Authentic:**
> *Of undisputed origin and not a copy.*

> **Genuine:**
> *Sincere.*

Throughout the book, I will reference bold, authentic and genuine in relation to Legendary Leadership and living a Technicolour Life. You might use different words to describe those sentiments and that is perfectly good too. The important aspect to this is that we both understand what I am referring to when you see these words.

You will also see references to this word.

Chameleon:
A person who changes their opinions or behaviour according to the situation.

It is not uncommon for people to flex in situations in order to fit in or not rock the boat. I describe this as being a chameleon; it's changing your colours to blend into the background. Being flexible is not a bad thing, but when you are choosing what colour to be based on what you think others want to see, then it is detrimental to you becoming the Legendary Leader of your Technicolour Life.

Many successful people, especially women in my experience, are doing really well on the face of it, but underneath the surface they don't feel successful. They've worked hard, broken through barriers and glass ceilings, but they are still left feeling significantly compromised. I call that living in the shades of grey (not *those* shades of grey!). When you step fully into who you are, it's like someone switched the TV from black and white to full-colour.

Being who you truly are is the key to Legendary Leadership and the first step to becoming that Legendary Leader. Remember, Legendary Leadership is not just about leading other people. First and foremost, it's about leading yourself in a life that you love. It's about applying your desire to do better and be better for yourself. Once you are operating as 100% yourself, not only do you feel in flow, others around you can feel it too. You become magnetic. From there, you become a Legendary Leader of others. This book is focused on that first part—becoming the Legendary Leader of your Technicolour Life for yourself.

Three Pillars of Legendary Leadership

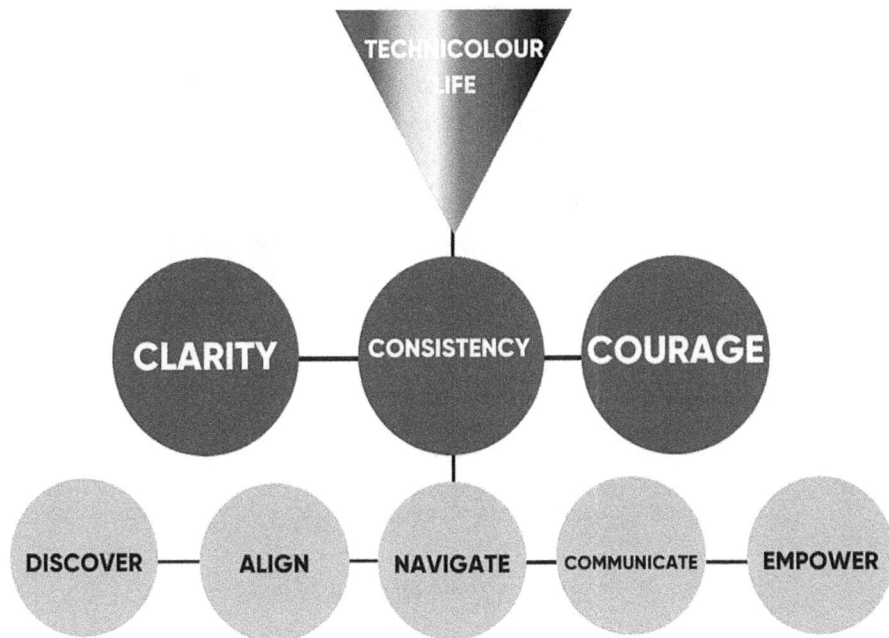

There are three key themes to becoming a Legendary Leader, but what underpins it all is Commitment.

> **Commitment:**
> *A pledge or promise; obligation.*

Commitment to doing what you can even when it is difficult or uncomfortable. Commitment to yourself and that you are worth the effort. Commitment to showing up and becoming a role model for others who dream of living their bold, authentic and genuine technicolour life.

TECHNICOLOUR ACTION: MY DECLARATION OF COMMITMENT TO MYSELF

In the coming pages and chapters, we're going to be doing a lot of work together. Some of it will come naturally and easily for you. Other parts you'll resist and have a natural tendency to put off or skip outright.

All of it matters.

All of it is designed to move you along towards your goals, toward accomplishing those things that are important to you. Together we'll be creating numerous tasks and assignments for you to work on, and **the things you resist doing are quite likely the things that are most important**: they'll be the stuff of you growing, reaching beyond what is already typically comfortable for you and into true expansion.

For this to work as best as it possibly can, we need for you to create a commitment to doing the work and staying true to the plans we make.

In short, I need for you to create for yourself that this work matters.

> *On a scale of 1 to 10, **without** yet having gone through it, how much do you trust this process to be worth doing?*
>
> *How committed are you to making this work?*
>
> *What's likely to prevent you from doing all of the work?*
>
> *What sort of things are you apt to put off or ignore?*
>
> *Are those things worth doing to get you what you want?*
>
> *What will you do when you're feeling stuck to get unstuck?*
>
> *How about if it's something you think is genuinely not worth doing?*

Thanks for bearing with this. The point of all of this is to provide a map for you to circle back to when the going gets tough.

Put this all together.

> *In a paragraph or three please summarize your commitment to doing the work: what's at stake for your efforts here, and what your strategy is for keeping on track.*

(Visit www.lorrainehamilton.net/purple-resources for a downloadable worksheet)

You will see reference to the following three themes often throughout the book—Commitment is what will deliver all three:

Clarity

Legendary Leaders know who they are. Clarity is multifaceted. The more clarity you have, the more authentic you can be.

Courage

Legendary Leaders are pioneers. They do what no-one else has ever done and that takes courage. Courage is about feeling uncomfortable and staying in the discomfort because you know it is going to be worth it.

Consistency

Legendary Leaders do what they say they will do. The more consistent you can be, the more of a safe environment you create, which allows everyone to be their best, especially you.

There are five steps that will contribute to these pillars.

Five Steps to Legendary Leadership

In the coaching field, we talk a lot about 'dancing in the moment with the client'. This is one of the fundamental principles that I teach my students in my coaching courses and DANCE is also the acronym for the steps that contribute to the whole process of Legendary Leadership.

1. Discover

You must be willing to dig deep into your own personal belief and values systems. This is where the bulk of my work is with private clients. It's also where the bulk of your own self-discovery work will be, which is reflected by the greater number of exercises in this section of the book.

2. Align

Living in alignment is what brings ease, joy and flow. When you have been living as a chameleon, it can be surprisingly tricky to achieve. Living in alignment is a practice. It takes time to apply what you *discover* to your life in a way that feels easeful. Just as you are really, really good at how you currently do life, you need to unlearn the ways that you are being and behaving that are not helpful, and replace them with new ways that inspire and energise you towards being the Legendary Leader of your Technicolour Life.

3. Navigate

Breaking out from your chameleon suit to live your Technicolour Life is scary—both consciously and unconsciously. You need a plan to make sure that you know where you are going and how to get there to make it easy to go the distance. The biggest threat to your new way of living is your old way of living. When life gets busy, humans revert back to what they know best, even if it is not what is best for them. The best way to ensure that you can stay on track is to know what your track looks like.

4. Communicate

Communication is at the heart of how we operate and succeed in life. When you begin to live in glorious technicolour, it can mean changing the way you interact with those around you. You need to know how to communicate consciously as you reintroduce yourself as the bold, authentic, genuine you. In this section of the book, you will discover that the first and most important communication path to work on is the communication you have within yourself in the form of emotions and beliefs.

5. Empower

In order to live as your true self all the time, you need to embody everything you have learned, including how to manage setbacks and challenges, as well as how to accept opportunities and praise. The sense of 'waiting to be found out' or not feeling good enough for opportunities or praise that come your way is hugely prevalent among the people I coach, yet so many of us do not share our stories because we feel shame about them. If you have ever felt like a fraud or an imposter or if you have ever felt that you would be judged if you revealed the real you, then this book is for you.

I wrote this book to show you that you can succeed in all areas of your life when you truly embrace who you are. More than that, it will make you stronger, bolder and more authentic. Truth be told, it's also *easier* and far less exhausting!

This book examines imposter syndrome or feeling like a fraud in a way that systematically dismantles the structures that have supported this feeling to the point where you may not know how else to live. It shares stories from women who are just like you; who are successful on the face of it, but have struggled with the same feelings. The information is presented in a fun but powerful way that reframes perspectives and dismantles the structures that may have been put in place so that you have *never* felt like you could show up as 100% yourself.

This book is not about dismantling the patriarchy, but it is about navigating your way through your own choices about how you want to show up in this evolving world. There has never been a better time to claim your life as your own and live it in glorious technicolour as the Legendary Leader you are.

This book is how.

Success is a verb, which means that doing the work, completing the exercises and engaging with the journal prompts will be so important to ensuring transformation by the end of this experience. Because this is more than a book; this is an opportunity for radical change. In each chapter, there will be lessons, stories and questions for you to answer or consider so that you can actually make change rather than just gather knowledge. Because while knowledge might be power, there are no results without action. I call these Technicolour Actions and Technicolour Tools, because you can pull them out and use them again and again. It's like having your very own toolkit for constructing your Technicolour Life.

If you truly want to live your boldest, most authentic, most genuine Technicolour Life and become the Legendary Leader you were born to be, then you are going to have to change what you are currently doing to elevate yourself to that next level.

Ready to begin?

"Being a geek is all about being honest about what you enjoy and not being afraid to demonstrate that affection. It means never having to play it cool about how much you like something. It's basically a licence to proudly emote on a somewhat childish level rather than behave like a supposed adult. Being a geek is extremely liberating."

~Simon Pegg

INTRODUCTION

The first time I dyed my hair, I did it to push people away. Now it is one of the things that attracts people to me. When I was 19 and at university, I dyed my waist-length blonde hair bright pink. In effect, it was part of a whole image that was designed to keep people at arm's length. I thought everyone would give me a wide berth if I looked strange. I didn't dye my hair because I was confident; I dyed my hair because I lacked confidence. In fact, at that time in my life, I was probably the least confident I had ever been.

I hadn't had the best experience at school and had been the subject of extensive bullying over an extended period of time. That experience never made sense to me. I didn't know why I'd been targeted for that kind of treatment from the bully and therefore couldn't take personal responsibility for it or make amends to remedy her problem with me. Looking back, the damage that was caused by that time in my life was not the hurt from the bully's actions, but that the world as I knew it was turned upside-down.

Up until that point, I believed that if I worked hard, I would get results; that if I was kind, others would be kind; that it was okay to make mistakes and learn from them; that if I took personal responsibility and apologised for mistakes, relationships could be repaired and things moved on.

The experience of bullying destroyed all that. There was no reason for my being targeted. (I actually know this to be true because I sat down with my bully 10 years afterwards and she told me so. She also apologised for her behaviour. I know that many people never get the opportunity to have this recourse with the person who has damaged them so deeply. If this is you, then please know that the great likelihood is that it wasn't about you, but about them.)

Not being able to identify why I was targeted meant that I formed a belief… If it had happened once, it could happen again. I simply did not feel equipped to deal with that again in my life.

Hence the crazy hair, the heavy metal clothes, the dark makeup. Anything that would put people off from getting close to me and then potentially hurting me.

Once I left university and entered the workforce, I stopped dyeing my hair, not because anyone told me I should, but because there was an expectation from everyone around me that I should 'fit in', that I should look 'professional'. And being the good girl that I was (and sometimes still am), I listened to them and did what was expected of me.

The thing is, though, I never felt like I fitted in. This misalignment within myself led to decades of bending and flexing to meet others' expectations. And it worked. I was arguably 'successful' in my professional career. I have a long, happy marriage and two teenage daughters who are doing well academically and expressing their artistic and sporting talents. I live in a beautiful house in a beach town in New Zealand and I have a passion for cars.

On the outside it looked like I had everything, so why didn't it feel like that on the inside?

Perhaps this sounds familiar.

You didn't work this hard, break through this many barriers, and smash this many ceilings to get where you are and feel so... *conflicted*.

On one hand, you're endlessly grateful for the bank balance, the 'dream' job, the leadership status, the house, the car... On the other hand, you feel guilty admitting that none of this brings you the true happiness and fulfilment you crave. (Not that you'd actually admit that out loud!)

It's as if you're putting on a chameleon's suit and going through the motions because that's what you were told to do by 'people who knew better'. And because ambition and achievement are in your blood, you've kept going. Climbing the corporate ladder is exciting, but it's also exhausting. And when the view from the top is grey and unworthy of all the personal sacrifices you've made to get there, you're left wondering:

Is it normal to feel dissatisfied when I have so much?

For people like you, yes. Success is natural for you, but it's come at the cost of pieces of yourself, a cost you're not prepared to pay any more. (Hint: you don't have to.)

Is it possible to become the leader of my life and find fulfilment in my work without completely starting over?

A-b-s-o-l-u-t-e-l-y. I've done it, as have hundreds of women (and a few brilliant men) who I've coached and educated.

How can I ditch this chameleon suit and bring 100% of me to my career, leadership and relationships?

So glad you asked! Because this book is going to answer that last little question and so much more. It is definitely worth sticking around because not only will I explain what to do and why, but also how. And I will equip you with everything you need in order to achieve Legendary Leadership in your Technicolour Life.

As an engineering leader turned executive coach and motivational speaker, I help high-achieving corporate climbers become Legendary Leaders of their Technicolour Lives, including their relationships and careers. If you want to join them, how about we switch up going through the motions and living in shades of grey for showing up as the boldest, brightest, and most authentic version of you and thriving in technicolour?

I might have wild hair, but you're in the steadiest of hands.

How to Get the Best from this Book

This book is a collection of teachings that will help you to understand why you are where you are and why you do what you do. There are also stories from my own experience, and those of my clients and colleagues to help you to see how these concepts work in reality and that you are not alone. And there are a number of exercises and journal prompts, which I strongly encourage you to complete as you work through the book.

The book is broken into chapters along the lines of the five steps to legendary leadership: Discover, Align, Navigate, Communicate, Empower. As you move through these chapters, you will see there is crossover between many of the steps. I have presented the information in a way that makes the most sense for you to work through on your own without having a coach alongside you. For example, the work that you do in the Discover and Align chapters may refer to how you communicate with yourself. Arguably, this could have been placed in the Communicate chapter but it is desirable to explore and examine it earlier.

This process is not a straight line. There is a difference between knowing and doing.

If you are anything like me then you will be thirsty for the knowledge contained within these pages. You have been taught to value knowledge and you can appreciate the purpose of the exercises provided. But how often do you promise yourself that you will come back to the exercises and prompts when you "have more time", or "can do them properly", or some other excuse? Trust me, I am the queen of this. Give me the knowledge. Just tell me the answer!

However, change comes from embodying the knowledge. It comes from getting out of your head and into your heart and gut. The virtue of actually taking the time to reflect, ponder, explore and complete the exercises is a quantum shift from reading a book. This is the closest you can get to having the type of transformational experiences my clients have when they work with me directly, so gift yourself the time and space to make the most of this resource in your hand.

In my group coaching program The Purple Hair Revolution, it is the participants who actually complete the worksheets and prompts that get the best results. The participants who are there for the community and knowledge certainly get that but they do not achieve as much as those who commit to taking imperfect action towards their goals.

Simply knowing is not enough to change your life from monochrome to glorious technicolour.

It took a monumental failure in my business, which I will share with you later, for me to realise that in my hurry to "be successful", I was missing the point entirely and operating from a knowing place rather than a doing place. Don't be me! It's exhausting and a waste of your time. I want more than that for you.

Give yourself some grace as you go through the work too. Some of what I suggest will be challenging and require you to be kind to yourself and vulnerable.

> *"People who wade into discomfort and vulnerability and tell the truth about their stories are the real badasses."*
>
> ~Brené Brown

Most people live their lives in the grey, bending to others' wills and expectations. This is your opportunity to break free from that mould and be who you are truly meant to be. That means gently exposing what the current reality is so that you can choose your new truth.

Throughout this book, you'll find a number of my favourite quotes from people who inspire me. These are phrases that I use often and share with my audience and clients to help them. One you will notice me coming back to again and again is this…

Change happens when we experience ourselves as successful and competent.

When we begin to see progress, it fuels us to make more progress, and more, and more. Wherever you can, notice that committing to doing this work, at whatever pace is right for you, is you being successful and competent. Give yourself as many opportunities to be successful and competent as you can.

CHAPTER ONE

Discover

"Vulnerability is not winning or losing; it's having the courage to show up and be seen when we have no control over the outcome. Vulnerability is not weakness; it's our greatest measure of courage."

~Brené Brown, *Rising Strong*

Over the years after university and in my corporate job, I kept trying to fit in, but I also wanted to be me. After a while, I started to dabble with colour again. When I was on maternity leave from my job, I dyed the underneath portion a vibrant-but-still-quite-conservative red colour which was nevertheless easy to hide. A few years later, I added a few purple highlights. A few years after that, I started to wear pink and purple extensions weaved into my hair. I still looked blonde overall, but there were these hints of colour. It took years for me to get to a point where I thought, *I want the bottom half at least of my hair to be purple* and began to wear it that way all the time. Today, it is two-thirds coloured in blue, pink and purple.

Every time I added more colour to my hair, it did bring more attention, but that is not why I was doing it. I was doing it to reflect on the outside who I was on the inside.

Today, my hair is what attracts many people to work with me. It's not a gimmick or a trick. It is a true reflection of who I am, a sign of authenticity, and that's what makes it work. I am comfortable in my hair, just as I am

1

comfortable in my body, my skin, my work and my family. In truth, *that* is what people find attractive, even if they can't quite put their finger on it.

Looking back, I wish I had dyed my hair purple sooner because it could have meant that I would be able to connect and help more people earlier. And that is what I mean when I ask...

What was your "Dye Your Hair Purple Sooner" moment?

When did you decide that you were not meant to stick the rules anymore, or that what you had been promised for making all the 'right' choices isn't what you ended up with?

You don't have to dye your hair purple to be a Legendary Leader. That's just what it took for *me* to feel empowered to be truly myself and recognise that it is in my power to be who I need to be to feel good in my skin.

In this chapter, you will uncover what makes you *you*. Years of fitting in and doing the right thing has disconnected us from who we were born to be. But it's not too late to Discover it once more.

Breaking Down the Walls to Find Clarity

As I mentioned in the introduction, there are three pillars to Legendary Leadership: Clarity, Consistency and Courage. The first pillar of Legendary Leadership is Clarity. In order for you to get enough clarity to live your Technicolour Life, we need to undo some very well-intentioned conditioning that has probably occurred as you were growing up. Because there is a very important piece of information that you need to know if you are feeling like you have lost your sense of self at this point in your life...

It is not your fault.

It is not your fault that you have unconscious beliefs and values running the show.

It is not your fault that you feel compelled to push yourself to breaking point in order to meet others' expectations of you.

It is not your fault that you need my help to unravel what has happened and get you on the right track for your future.

Relax, your guilt has no place here.

When we are born, we are all blank canvases. We need others to tell us how to behave and what is expected of us. As babies and children, we look to those around us to inform how we fit in and how we belong. It has to be that way. And at its core, this is how we survive.

If you are anything like me, you have been a great student and employee throughout your career. It's important for you to do your best. Note, I didn't say *be* the best, but *do* your best. Maybe you were in the top 5-10% of your class or you progressed well through your career, achieving promotions and opportunities, but in a quieter, more understated way than some of your colleagues.

When the rules are clear, you know how to excel. Perhaps you are not the most confident or extroverted, but you know how to meet or exceed expectations. Or you could be extroverted and confident in some aspects of your life, but you find that playing a part is exhausting and drains you for other parts of your life. And lastly, there's a possibility that you're just so busy doing all the things to the best of your ability that you haven't had time to stop and even check in to see if they are still what you want most in your life.

The most common problem I see is when my clients have moved on in their head logically, but are still operating unconsciously from a set of beliefs and values that no longer serve them.

This is where you need clarity through redefining success and choosing the values that will best support you in your pursuit of it.

TECHNICOLOUR ACTION: WHAT CHANGE DO YOU WANT FOR YOURSELF?

Now is the time to break out a new journal and grab your favourite pen, make a cup of something comforting or pour a glass of wine, and really dig deep into what you want from your experience of this book. And it is an experience. The purpose of this book is to change you in some way: from where you are now to who you want to be when you have finished reading.

What do you want from taking the time to read and experience this book?

How do you want to be different after reading this book?

Why do you want it?

We will build on this as you move through the chapters. Take a moment to write something down now though, as it will serve as a focus or beacon as you move through the rest of the book. It is perfectly natural to not know the answer right now, but I encourage you to not skip this first exercise. This may be your first experience of taking imperfect action towards an outcome. I sincerely believe and hope that it will not be your last.

DYE YOUR HAIR PURPLE SOONER MOMENT: KARLEY

The moment I realised my personal and professional success were inextricably linked was when I noticed that I was applying what I learned as an athlete to my business. I started recording videos called Lessons from the Trail for business owners. The point of those videos was about being on the trail, barrelling downhill, not paying attention to where you're going. It's easy to go in the wrong direction or pick up too much momentum and land on your face. This metaphor translates to business. Momentum is great; too much momentum is not.

I also realised that periodised training was relevant. As athletes, we break things down for our big races and reverse-engineer our program. We do that in business too. We know what our ultimate goal is and work backwards from there. Periodised training looks at the whole season, instead of race by race, or goal by goal. You've got a base-building period, where you're preparing and getting ready. You've got a speed-building period, where you focus on specific skills. Then you've got down season. I find that most business owners don't practice that last one—the downtime—and end up fatigued.

I was in a mastermind meeting when it occurred to me that business owners were saying the exact same thing as athletes—that they're burnt out. Of course, I immediately saw more parallels between athletes and business owners: they are competitive, driven, high-paced and don't know how to slow down.

In relation to burnout and identity, anger comes into the picture. Growing up playing with boys and possibly because of my own orientation floating near the middle of the gender spectrum, I internalised the expression of anger over tears. In the burnout phase of retiring from sport, the hardest part for me was dealing with the loss of identity. And I mean identity through my whole life: from being groomed as a figure skater and having to be feminine and polite and proper to being judged on and off the ice, from coming out to fitting in, from being very young in business to moving to an unknown city and building a network. Throughout my life, I found myself moulding to the identity other people wanted me to be.

Growing up in a heteronormative household, life expects you to grow up and get married and wear a white dress and have kids. Having a gender-fluid essence to my being, I figured myself out around the age of 18 and really struggled through the coming out process. I've always shown a chameleon identity to be able to be in the safe zone. When I'm on stage, I'm comfortable being feminine but it's almost like it's expected. It's easier. I'm different, but I can pass. I recognise that so many people can't and it breaks my heart, because I know the pain of having hurtful words thrown at you.

Watching other women in the community who were more butch, I realised being more feminine was an easier way to pass and be accepted—in my case to make money, to have a business. I didn't put up barriers that people would have to get through in order to accept me and want to work with me. I just became what they wanted.

I decided I was going to be me when I moved out to Vancouver and dug into my career. I took on a business partner at 28 and hired a business coach at 32. I remember sitting down with my coach in our first session and having a complete and utter meltdown. I was in tears before I could open my mouth. I said, "I'm 32 years old and I live in one of the most beautiful cities in the world. I own real estate and a business that's moving quickly up the ranks. I have a great reputation in the city. I'm dating a bombshell. My life should be fantastic and I'm fucking miserable." And he said, "Okay, the work starts here."

I realised that by navigating the world as a chameleon and fitting into everybody else's boxes, I had moved away from me. I had buffered my boldness. I had worked myself into this box of what everybody else wanted me to be.

Together with my coach, I took it all apart piece by piece then. What's my purpose? What do I value? What are my values? I discovered the reason I was miserable. In my business, my business partner was a fantastic person, but our values weren't aligned. It kept pushing us apart and I couldn't do it anymore. In my personal life, the woman I was dating was 40 years old and I was the first woman she had dated, but again our values and life experiences weren't aligned.

Here's the beauty of this story. As I was dissolving my business and rebuilding myself, I built the foundation of what came next. This was how I learned to build brands, because I was trialling it on myself. I realised that a brand is ultimately an expression of who we truly are. I wanted to work with individuals who were building their personal brand and I developed my system, the Surefire Strategy.

Raising a daughter, parents might expect to throw her wedding or hold her children, but in the time and place where I was, gays couldn't marry. For me, the hardest thing in coming out was disappointing my family. As I stepped into my hopes and dreams, I had to give up some of those hopes and dreams too, because I had bought into their story. In the same way, when I burnt out as an athlete, I had to grieve for the loss of the story I had built for myself that I was aiming for the Olympics. I don't know that I ever actually wanted that for myself, but if I wasn't going to become a professional athlete, all I was doing in my twenties was effing around on a bike for fun according to everybody else.

> When you choose to be yourself, you're choosing to say no to what everybody else expects of you.
>
> **Karley Cunningham, Big Bold Brand**

The Success Myth

While some adventures are better when you don't know what's going to happen or where you're going to end up, for this adventure I'd like us to have an idea of what the endpoint looks like, or at least what you believe the endpoint might look like if you were there today.

Collectively, we have a very messed-up view of success. This is because we've spent years or decades allowing other people and the media to dictate what success is, means or looks like. But have you ever stopped to think about what success actually means? We are constantly being fed messages and images of what society, the media, our families, institutions, and so on deem to be success:

- *Top job*
- *Six-figure salary*
- *Seven-figure business*
- *Size 10 body*
- *Youthful appearance*
- *Happy, healthy children*
- *Nutritious family meals*
- *Clean, tidy, organised home*
- *Amazing sex life*
- *Happy, thriving relationship with a significant other*
- *Exciting and supportive friends*
- *Regular vacations*
- *Being fit and healthy*
- *Contributing to your community*

And because it is being constantly impressed upon us with no conscious challenge, we set about getting on with it. After all, we're not afraid of hard work, are we? We're prepared to take responsibility for our own results, so we get to work on all... the... things. But at what cost?

In today's hectic reality, burnout and adrenal fatigue are two terms that are thrown around almost as badges of honour. Whatever you prefer to call it, we've all seen how stress has become a constant drain on our energy. And yet, judging by the way we relate to it, sometimes it says, "Look how busy, hardworking and driven I am." However, our modern-day obsession with running ourselves into the ground—like it's a good thing—makes no sense. There are no awards for being the most exhausted!

One thing is for sure: collectively, we are feeling more stressed than ever before.

Back in 2014, I reached a point where I was in a position to buy my dream car, a SAAB 9-3 convertible. It wasn't a new car, but had been my dream car since 1999. Back in 1999, I had come really close to owning one as a company car for my engineering role, because my company gave me a car allowance that I could use on any car I wanted. I went to the dealership and fell in love with a silver version with a navy blue hood. It was gorgeous. I took back all the information that the dealer gave and I began to crunch some numbers. I could get the car, but it was going to mean supplementing the allowance considerably each month out of my own funds. At the time, I was single with no kids and I really didn't need a car that big. I kept looking and ended up with a smaller, cheaper silver convertible with a blue hood that actually cost less than my allowance each month. It was the sensible choice and I took it, but I always dreamed of owning that SAAB.

Come 2014, I was in a position where I didn't need to have the family seven-seater anymore. I could have the car I wanted. (Incidentally, I still have the family seven-seater and a 1966 MG Midget. I have a thing for cars it would seem!) I set to work trying to find the SAAB convertible that I had my heart set on. Eventually, I came across one and I was besotted. It was high-gloss black with a gunmetal grey interior and I couldn't contain my excitement as I counted down the days until I could drive it. I flew up to Auckland to pick it up and I was so excited to get to the dealership and get behind the wheel. There were a couple of scratches on it that hadn't been so clear on the photos, but nothing could dampen my excitement to get behind the wheel and drive it the eight hours home.

As the sun began to set and the roads became dark, I switched the head-lights on, but nothing happened. I was still a couple of hours from home and the roads in New Zealand are not the brightly lit motorways I was used to driving on when I'd lived and grown up in Europe. It was getting really hard to see the road in front of me. The excitement of the day gave way to intense concentration and getting home in one piece.

Ever the optimist, I carried on and figured it would be a small thing; that we'd fix it and look forward to a summer of top-down cruising. Well, I got home in one piece, but it turned out that the headlights were just the start. The control for the electric passenger seat broke in my hand on that first night too. Both headlights weren't affixed to the casings. And within a few days, the power steering also failed while I was negotiating a round-about. Then, the convertible roof started leaking fluid over me whenever I turned a corner, finally jamming halfway open.

That car broke my heart.

How could a car break my heart?

Well, it wasn't the car. It was what the car represented to me. I had wrapped up so much meaning into a 10-year-old vehicle. The 'idea' of the car represented success to me. It represented reclaiming a prior missed opportunity. It represented freedom and elevation from being a responsible mum. It represented success and achievement on a number of levels. And when it turned out to be so desperately broken, my idea of these things was broken too.

Funnily enough, my go-to thought process was not to be frustrated and angry with the car or the dealership, but frustrated and angry with myself. That might sound familiar to you. My clients often report that they have lost their sense of themselves as they pursue the supposed tenets of happiness. They achieve the seemingly impossible and have most or all of the things on the list of what the media tells us makes us successful. Then they realise that it hasn't actually brought them happiness at all. They've been sold a lemon, like my car. This induces intense feelings of guilt and shame. On the face of it, they have succeeded, so they feel like they would appear ungrateful if they complained; after all, there are so many who have so much less.

When I look at the root of all of this stress and unhappiness, the answer becomes simple. It's about redefining what success means... *to you.*

It's not about the thing. It's about what the thing represents to us. In my car example, the car represented a lot of things to me: having something I wanted rather than something practical, choosing myself, unfinished business, and reaching a goal. The representations don't have to make sense to anyone but you. The point is each aspect was associated with a feeling. A feeling of pride, excitement, joy and so on. Someone else could look at the same car and have a whole host of other feelings, or even be completely ambivalent.

We don't want the thing. We want the feeling that we associate with the thing.

The truth is that your version of success is unique to you.

DYE YOUR HAIR PURPLE SOONER MOMENT: ANNA

It's ironic the way life sometimes thrusts you in a direction that you are perhaps too scared to venture down yourself. After returning to a busy corporate marketing role when my daughter and second child was 10 months old, I felt I was conquering the world. Yet, 15 months into that journey of commuting and working hard, I was facing a diagnosis of adrenal fatigue and suffering from anxiety. I knew that something in our lives must change and the tiny voice in the back of my head was telling me this was not how it's meant to be.

I resigned from my marketing role, leaving behind the security of a great job and a team that I truly enjoyed working with. I knew when I was leaving that I was setting up my own marketing consultancy, yet I still felt like a total failure who was unable to juggle the demands of work and motherhood. I spent at least two months stabilising my health and working through the feelings of failure that my perfectionist self was thrusting upon me. Yoga, counselling and working on projects with clients slowly led me to the realisation that perhaps I could make this work for myself and my family as a boss mama.

Nearly a year into the journey of being self-employed, fighting hard to find my niche and new business and constantly battling the internal thoughts that I am not good enough, I can honestly say that I wished I'd had the guts to do this sooner. Does the doubt go away? No! But I feel I have grown so much in myself. I have been forced to put myself out there, learn new skills and grow in confidence. Was I ready for this step? Again, no. It was almost like my body and health forced me in this direction. It made me review my own values and how I was living life. Nature is amazing in that way because it forces you to stop and listen sometimes.

When my second child was a baby, I had thought about trying to go out on my own and create some work for myself, but I talked myself out of it saying it simply wasn't possible and I didn't have the support networks in place. Do I wish I'd been braver sooner? Sometimes. Equally, I've learnt over many years that everything is in good time. While I wish this realisation had come sooner, I also recognise it came when it was needed the most and when I was ready to embrace the small possibility that I was worth it.

I've had to reprogram my own definition of success. I still work on this every day when I find myself judging myself. Success should not be a job title or money earnt, but the moments I get to spend with my family, the new skills and the amazing people I get to work with in collaboration. I am so pleased I had the nudge to give it a crack working for myself.

If only it came sooner......

Anna Colville-Smith, mum, marketer and business owner

I hope you see just how unique you are, and how unique everyone else is. It simply doesn't make sense for us all to have the same measures of success.

This is also the reason that living your life in glorious technicolour and being 100% you is so damn hard. We might excel when we know the rules of the game, but when all we have is choice, it can be scary. Choice can be good, but choice also makes us question ourselves. What if we make the 'wrong' choice or decision? How will we know when we have succeeded? Who will tell us that we are on the right path? When we know the rules of the game, we usually know what choices to make, but when you are the rule maker, it can feel scary to make choices without external input or validation.

The answer is setting success markers for yourself. I am here to help you do that, so that you can build in the certainty you need that you are taking the right steps.

I'm not promising that you won't make mistakes along the way. In fact, you definitely will sometimes! It's part of the learning process. But know this… There is no failure, only feedback.

You may have an idea of what you want your life to look like; that's probably why you bought this book. But you may also still have questions like…

What will other people think if I follow my true path?

Shouldn't I just be grateful for what I have?

Isn't it wrong to want <insert your deepest desires here>?

Let's start at the beginning: knowing yourself first and foremost. Because when *you* know yourself, no-one can say you're on the wrong track.

DYE YOUR HAIR PURPLE SOONER MOMENT: CAROLINE

I am not a holding-onto-regrets kind of person, but I could have embraced my uniqueness earlier, and stopped trying to fit into a mould of what success looked like, or maintaining the image of what I was "supposed" to be based on my career. Fundamentally, I wish I had disconnected my worth from my achievements, and my self-image from my education.

When I stopped worrying about making other people uncomfortable with my incongruent (to them) interests and talents, I noticed that my confidence soared. I never thought I cared much about what people thought, but apparently I did, because I was embarrassed to share my tangential projects and interests in my professional circles. I knew that their confusion or lack of support was their own insecurity reflecting back to me. Also, I didn't want to feel scrutinized, like a bug in a science exhibit, because people were always so curious about what I was doing. It didn't feel like a good kind of curious, but the "can't look away" kind of curious.

When I started owning my ambition, drive and interests, I noticed that it gave others permission to do the same. I have never been one to shy away from risks. Taking a risk to be completely unapologetic about my life and the unconventional path I have taken has helped me learn more empathy for others who are struggling to do the same. I am confident that my regret-proof life only comes from taking those risks and chances.

I host events called Comfort Zone Challenges, so I relate to that feeling and embrace it daily. I am very familiar with how I embrace discomfort. It is the feeling of facing ambiguity, which is one of the topics I deliver as a keynote public speaker.

For me, the physical feeling can be like bouncing on tiptoes, or watching a tennis ball go back and forth internally. I can also get a dry mouth, purse my lips slightly, and get tension in my jaw. This feeling is the same whether I'm at the top of a mountain ready to ski down a challenging run, picking up the phone for an uncomfortable conversation, stepping onto a comedy stage to perform stand-up, or pressing "buy" on that solo round-the-world ticket. It's the feeling of accepting uncertainty and moving forward anyway. It's a feeling of "here we go!" It's a feeling of excitement mixed with a tinge of fear, which helps push me forward into new challenges.

Comfort is an illusion. Comfort is a pit-stop on the way to magnificence. Sometimes it's nice, but sometimes temporary discomfort is the secret golden ticket to a regret-proof life. An example might be when I bombed on stage. Apparently, every comic bombs, but it doesn't feel good. I was hosting a comedy fundraiser event, but of the 150 people or so there, only about 8 were listening to my set, and they were friends and the organizers. Everyone else was chatting or eating. It was humiliating. But why? I didn't die. I didn't lose my job or livelihood. Rejection is as painful as physical pain.

Even though I bombed, I was still the person on stage. I was still the person sharing my creativity with full vulnerability to the world. I was still learning. So, I finished my set and told myself that the fear was an illusion. I did not fail.

The next time I hosted an event, it was so much better thanks to what I'd learned at the fundraiser. That experience gave me the confidence to know that I can handle failure, bounce back and try again. Isn't that the actual definition of resilience?

Caroline Brookfield, veterinarian and creativity mentor

Identifying Your Unique Stress Strategy

Stress is such a massive component of our daily lives that I want to address it right here at the beginning. That way, over the course of the rest of the book, you will be in the best possible shape to get the most from what I have to share.

Picture this…

Three days into the March 2020 COVID-19 lockdown, I stood in the kitchen of my house with my mouth agape. I had just witnessed the most amazing exchange between my 15-year-old and my husband. What started out as a simple statement from our daughter that she was going to bake a cake degenerated into an all-out verbal war with doors slamming, eyes rolling, screams, accusations and threats in a matter of seconds. I mean, these guys are absolute pros at pushing each other's buttons!

So there I was, left standing in the middle of the kitchen having gone from excitedly planning the next four weeks, imagining us coming out the other side being the Best Family Ever, more closely bonded and feeling such gratitude to have this family time just as our kids are growing up and stretching their wings away from us… to—BOOM!—being on my own in the room, wondering what in the world just happened!

Lockdown was stressful. Am I right? And 'stress' looks so different for everyone.

My husband was stressed about what the lockdown meant for his business. My daughter was stressed about not seeing her friends and what the impact of coronavirus really was going to be. I was stressed about witnessing the interaction between them and what that meant for the future weeks and months ahead.

There are many different triggers that cause us to feel stress and there are many different ways that we can respond to those stressful feelings. My husband and daughter demonstrated their stress feelings by arguing and slamming doors. I demonstrated my feelings of stress by retreating to my office. At another time, I might have demonstrated my stress feelings by pouring a glass of wine, or reaching for the chocolate.

Our stress triggers and responses make us unique. And all of this stress just bubbles away under the surface of the superficial actions that we move through day-to-day. In this example, the activity seemed innocuous, but the reaction was unexpected. When my daughter announced that she was taking over the kitchen to bake, what my husband was thinking had nothing to do with the baking. However, the fact that so many things were out of his control caused him to make a stress-fuelled comment, and his comment was enough to ignite a stress-fuelled explosion in our 15-year-old! What was going on there was stress. And lots of it!

The first step of the Discover part of Legendary Leadership is learning how to manage your own stress before you try to lead others, because managing stress will have a huge impact on your ability to be Clear, Consistent and Courageous. When we are stressed, our ability to process information is compromised by up to 80%. Another way to think about it is that we drop up to four educational grade levels when we are stressed. Can you imagine your response to situations when you were four educational grade levels below where you are now? That's like going from your Bachelor's degree to primary school! How well did you respond to stress when you were a child of primary school age?

We are bombarded with information all... the... time. But I don't mean information like emails, social media, news, advertising, etc. What I mean is that we are being bombarded by sensory information. At any given moment, we are consciously, and more often subconsciously, assessing our surroundings to ensure that we are safe. *What's that noise? What was that movement I caught out of the corner of my eye? Is it too hot or cold? How does that taste? Is it safe or is it poisonous?*

We make a *huge* number of judgements at the same time. We are constantly deleting, distorting or vastly generalising the information just so we can keep on top of it, but how do we determine what to keep, what to delete, what to distort and what to generalise? The answer is filters. We have a number of filters that we use to make our judgements.

We use the filter of our values—what is most important to us in life?

We use the filter of our belief system—what do we believe about certain situations or people?

We use a filter based on our memories—and our memories are not always to be relied on, but we still use them to filter!

We use a filter of past experiences and past decisions—the output of previous experiences is a quick way to filter information into the keep, delete, distort or generalise buckets.

And we use a filter of strategies.

Let's talk about those strategies for a moment…

We have a strategy for everything we do: getting out of bed in the morning, getting dressed, making a purchase; everything. Have you ever tried to shower differently? We have a strategy for showering!

We even have a strategy for getting stressed.

The output of all of those filters means that every one of us is having a completely unique experience right now. Even though there are a number of commonalities that have brought us to this same book at this same moment in time, we are all using our filters to 'code' it differently. By 'coding', I mean we attach our own unique meaning to the experience, and we will have a feeling attached to that meaning.

How are you feeling right now? What do you notice about what you are thinking as you read? Perhaps this is all new information to you. You might be feeling interested, curious, and eager to learn more. Those feelings will cause you to be focused on the book in your hands, eyes open and energised to find out more. If this is not new information to you, or I haven't done a good job of making it easy to see yourself in this scenario, you might be feeling frustrated, bored or even annoyed. That will cause your body language, attention, focus or behaviour to be a bit different. Perhaps you are only reading with half of your attention, or you are doing something else at the same time.

Your thoughts, feelings and behaviour are all inextricably linked and that link determines your results. If you want to change your results, any results, you need to change your behaviour or the actions that you are taking.

One of the key pieces of my work is for patients of weight loss surgery. A long history of dieting breaks the mind-body connection. Dieters are literally taught to ignore the feelings in their body in order to lose weight. And it is not just dieters. We are all being encouraged to ignore our body's signals and information. Think about Nike's "Just Do It" slogan, being told to "just push through", Susan Jeffers trademarking the phrase "feel the fear and do it anyway". All of these messages, while seemingly harmless on the surface, are actually telling us to ignore what we feel.

Those feelings and meanings will determine what you do next. And it is the *action* you take that will determine your results.

Let's come back to this idea that we have our own unique strategy for getting stressed, because most conflict stems from stress. One important aspect of being the Legendary Leader of your bold, authentic, genuine life, perhaps the *most* important aspect of personal leadership, is keeping calm so that you can make good decisions. Remember, stress can compromise your ability to process information by up to 80%, so even if you have the best information, without a cool head to process it, you can make bad decisions. Often, we don't even know we are stressed until it's too late. We're in the primary school level of thinking before we realise it!

Imagine, if you can, a mum and her toddler in the supermarket. They're in the middle of the frozen food aisle when Mum bumps into her friend and they start chatting and catching up. After a minute or so, the toddler starts to get bored and begins to say, "Mum, Mum, Mum." Mum continues on with her conversation. After getting no response, the toddler increases her volume a little bit, "Mum, Mum, Mum!" Mum still continues to catch up with her friend. They're talking about the concern they have for another friend in their circle. Next, the toddler starts to get a bit more urgent, "MUM, MUM, MUUUUUM!" Mum continues to chat, so now the toddler is going hard for attention and starts to tug and pull on Mum's trouser legs while chanting, "MUM, MUM, MUUUUUUUUUM!" Still nothing, so the toddler's stress levels are through the roof and she drops to the floor and starts to thrash and wail in an all-out tantrum. Mum looks round and goes, "How on earth did that happen?"

It's the same with our stress strategy.

First, there are the whispers that something needs our attention. If we ignore those whispers, they begin to get louder. If we ignore them again, they get louder still. And louder and louder until we are having a physical equivalent of a toddler tantrum.

And that can be pretty scary!

Think about a time when you felt really, really stressed. What are some of the physical symptoms you experienced? Perhaps they included:

Increased heart rate
Shallow breathing
Palpitations
Headache
Clenched jaw
Blurred vision
Shaking

None of that sounds like a party, right? And how many stories have you heard about people taking themselves off to hospital or phoning an ambulance because they thought they were having a heart attack, only to be told that it was stress or a panic attack? This is not funny. When you feel like this, you are not in the best shape to make decisions. In fact, feeling this way can lead you to make decisions that sabotage your success, not shape it. The problem is that we have spent years or even decades disconnecting our minds from our bodies so we don't hear the first whispers that something needs our attention. We only start to listen when the symptoms are scary and we are already in a state of stress that severely compromises our ability to make good decisions.

What would happen if we could hear those messages sooner? The earlier you can detect the messages, the more time you have to recognise that something needs your attention and the more control and choice you have as to how you will respond. The earlier you can identify the whispers, the calmer you can stay and the better leader you become.

Legendary Leaders can self-manage to the point where they are able to identify their early stress symptoms and treat them as messages to pay attention to something. They stop, assess and remove themselves from the stress so they have the benefit of perspective when deciding what to do next.

DYE YOUR HAIR PURPLE SOONER MOMENT: RB

RB is CEO of a digital marketing agency. He runs a large team and is responsible for bringing in enough sales to be profitable as well as pushing the boundaries of cutting edge technologies to ensure that his clients are always being seen in their digital channels.

When I worked with RB, we did a lot of work on stress management. One of the most memorable sessions that we completed was where I taught him how to manipulate the stressful situations he had to manage so that they didn't cause him to show that stress to his wider team.

By using the technique of distancing himself from the stressful situation, he gained perspective and was a lot more consistent around his team. This meant he created a safe space for his team to be the best that they could be. It gave him an enormous amount of confidence in being able to deal with any stresses that came up.

TECHNICOLOUR TOOL: CHECKING IN

Practice checking in with how you are feeling several times a day.

What physical feelings can you identify?

What messages do you think those feelings are trying to convey?

What changes, if any, do you need to make in response to those messages?

Let's begin to set the foundation for your version of success by turning everything on its head!

Turn Your Goals on Their Head

In the Navigate chapter of this book, I will introduce you to a goal-setting framework that *actually* works, but first we need to discover an important shift so that you can redefine success: from doing to being.

In my younger days when I allowed a bully to shape a large portion of who I was, I wish I'd known how to shift my perspective. It took me years and some excellent therapy to get to a point where I could loosen the rigid world view and look differently at situations, other people, and the world. It has been, quite simply, life-changing. It's amazing how a belief that seemed so concrete can crumble when looked at from just a slightly different angle. Now I happily spend my life helping people to see their situations from a different perspective so that they can feel differently about it. And you can do it too.

Our results are based on the actions we take, but the actions we take are dependent on how we feel about a situation. If we want to change our results, we need to change how we feel.

In this conversation with former client, Susan, we discussed a challenge she was facing in her business.

> *Me: What do you want to be different?*
>
> *Susan: I want more time for me. I want to be less stressed.*
>
> *Me: What do you need to do to have that?*
>
> *Susan: I need to make more money so I can hire more staff. I need to find more leads.*
>
> *Me: And once you've found more leads, hired the right staff and made more money, how will you be different?*
>
> *Susan: I'll be more relaxed and able to see the wood for the trees... I'll be more confident that I can handle whatever comes at me... I'll be organised and able to plan for growth...*
>
> *Me: And if you were all those things now—relaxed, confident, organised and able to plan for growth—would it make it easier to find more leads, hire the right staff and make more money?*
>
> *Susan: Yes!*
>
> *Me: Okay, can you see that by setting goals around being more relaxed, confident and organised, it will be easier to do the things you need to do in order to have what you want to have?*

Susan: I guess.

Me: Let's focus on those things first, because when you feel relaxed, confident and organised, everything else will feel a whole lot easier.

Susan: I get it! Alright, let's do it!

It's clear to see how Doing leads to the sense of Being. However, when you focus on Being relaxed, confident and organised, the Doing becomes much easier and the goal of having more time and being less stressed is almost a by-product of that. This approach flies in the face of the way that many of us have been brought up.

Let's go back to the beginning.

When we are born we are a blank canvas. We need to be trained how to behave. Generally, this looks like certain behaviour being either rewarded or penalised. That is how we learn what is acceptable and what is not. As you are reading this book, I suspect you are very good at this approach.

This pattern follows on into our school careers. We behave a certain way and we are either rewarded (with good grades, awards, opportunities, etc.) or penalised (exam failures, rework, suspension or expulsion).

As we move into the workforce, the pattern continues with a little added complexity as now we are working to earn money. Money leads to us having the necessities of life and luxuries. Once again though, we behave a certain way and are either rewarded (pay rise, promotions, opportunities, bonuses) or penalised (performance management, redundancy, discipline). One route takes us closer to our goals and dreams, whereas the other takes us further away.

In this description, we are always chasing the rewards from which we set the goal.

For example: I will work hard so that I can make money and then take a trip so that I can be relaxed, happy and successful. That introduces a further question: if you were relaxed, happy and successful would it change the way you showed up? The answer is most likely yes.

The problem is we have been conditioned throughout our life to chase the reward, to always be headed towards the carrot, whereas the key to living a bold, genuine, authentic life is to make decisions and take action as if you are already there.

What Success *Really* Looks Like

Earlier in this chapter, I invited you to jot down what you wanted to get from this book and why you wanted it. Now is the time to think a bit deeper about this. I have shown you that we do not often want the thing we are working towards, but the feeling that the thing will give us. If we focus more on how we are Being, it can help us in Doing what we need to do in order to be successful.

Early on in my coaching career, I had a client called Stephen, a young father who had had a successful rugby career and now worked in a bank to provide for his family. He was strong and capable. In his early thirties though, he was diagnosed with multiple sclerosis, a disease that was disabling his spinal cord and brain, making everyday tasks more and more difficult.

When I met Stephen, he was taking a medication to slow the progress of the disease through regular injections. At first, everything was going well, but over time Stephen began to develop a phobia to the needles used to inject his medicine. There was no other way for him to take the medication, so what had been a simple procedure turned into a scenario where two district nurses would spend half a day with Stephen trying to get him into a headspace for them to administer the injection. Imagine a still-strong former rugby player having to be held down by two other people to have this weekly injection. I spent two sessions with Stephen getting to know him and what motivated him. Midway through the second session, he took his injection himself with no fuss, no preamble, nothing.

What was different? Stephen's perspective had changed. Through getting to know him, I had realised that he was a swimming teacher for kids in his spare time and that teaching was in his DNA. By simply reframing his circumstances to being a role model for kids who had to take injections for their health, the way he felt about his own situation shifted a full 180 degrees and he was able to move past an incredibly debilitating phobia.

And if Stephen can do it, you can do it too.

TECHNICOLOUR ACTION: BEING A TECHNICOLOUR ME

Look back at what you want to get from this book and further develop that in light of what you have learned so far.

Think back to a time when you felt unstoppably bold, genuine, authentic, and everything seemed to be in glorious technicolour:

What were you doing?

Who were you with?

How were you feeling?

How do you need to Be to make it easier to Do what you need to do?

What would be a resourceful state for you to be in right now?

When my clients come to me, they usually have specific goals in mind. Those might be around building their confidence so that they can charge more for their services, losing weight and feeling more motivated about being healthy, or taking the next step in their career. It doesn't matter what the goals is exactly. What matters is that they are feeling stuck. And you might be feeling stuck right now too.

The problem isn't that you are stuck per se. It's that we're not looking at the whole picture. "Work-life balance" is a term that has become common over the past decade or so. Personally, I'm not a fan. Assuming that we are either at work or otherwise doing life outside of work is misleading on a number of levels. First, your work or career is a part of your life. Second, there are lots of parts to your life. And finally, balance suggests that the relationship between these parts is static. So I'm calling time on "work-life balance" in favour of a "blended life".

Our lives are a rich tapestry of all sorts of priorities. Work or career is one of them, but there are plenty of others too. And if we don't pay attention to them all, they suffer.

The Technicolour Life Wheel allows you to check in on a number of aspects of your life and see how they are working together. It's not about having a perfect life; it's about the blend.

TECHNICOLOUR ACTION: A BLENDED LIFE

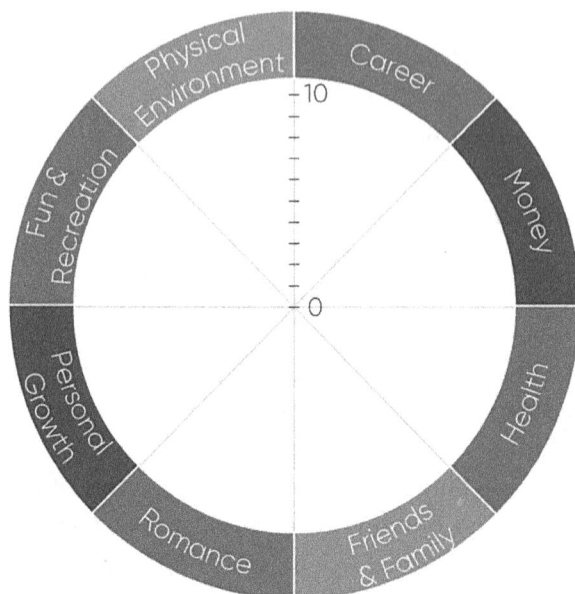

Give each area a score out of 10 for your level of current satisfaction. For example, if you are 100% happy in your career, then score it 10. If you couldn't be less happy, score it 1.

Go ahead and do that for all the sections. Be deliberate in your scoring. Think about how you know to give an area the score you are giving it. For example, if you score Fun and Recreation a 5, how do you know it's a 5 and not 4 or 6?

A word on 7s. I have a business coach who refuses to allow me to score anything a 7. This is a practice that I have taken into my own work with clients too. The reason being that 7 is a cop-out, middle of the road and non-committal. Whenever you want to score something 7, think extra hard. Is it a soft 7, which is really a 6, or a solid 7 which could really be an 8?

The point of the Technicolour Life Wheel is not to have every area at 10. It's to create equity across all areas of your life. Imagine if you were rolling the wheel that you have created through your scores down the road. Would the wheel roll smoothly, or would it be a very bumpy ride? If your wheel is pretty bumpy, that suggests there are areas of your life you are not satisfied with. This can lead to living a life in grayscale. A lower score can indicate that you are not living up to your own expectations in that area, which causes you to be less than 100% yourself.

When you are clear on how things are now, you can begin to look at ways to bring more alignment into your life, which we will look at in the next chapter. But that's not the whole picture. We are just at the beginning of creating the awareness that will lead to the clarity you need to live a Technicolour Life. Next, we are going to take a look at your values, or what matters to you most.

Using Values as Your Guiding Light

When we get on a plane, we trust the pilot to get us safely to our destination. Imagine if the pilot was flying the plane with a blindfold on. How confident would you be that you would reach your destination safely? I'm guessing not very!

You are the pilot of your life. When you don't know your values, it is like flying with a blindfold on. You are flying blind. Values are non-negotiable when you want to become the Legendary Leader of your Technicolour Life. Even if my clients have done a lot of personal development work before and tell me that they know what their values are, I insist that they work through a values process with me as part of our first three coaching sessions. Why? Because after working with hundreds of clients, more often than not, I find clients become stuck because their values are out of alignment.

So, what *are* values?

Values are your lifestyle priorities or preferences. They are one of the ways that you make judgements on how you will interact with the world and people. Collectively, I like to call them my moral compass. They inform what I do and how I do it to be 100% me.

My values are my motivating factors. If what I am doing is aligned with my values (like writing this book is aligned with creativity, honesty, achievement and challenge), then goals become easeful and fun. When I try to do something that is not aligned with my values, then goals become difficult or damn near impossible!

DYE YOUR HAIR PURPLE SOONER MOMENT: SARAH-JAYNE

I had a lot going on when that Eureka moment occurred. I remember it vividly. I was sitting in a little French café in Tauranga, New Zealand, tearing pieces off my almond croissant, at a meeting with a business coach. I was doing an exercise, checking in on how I was feeling about my life, not just my business. I remember looking at my percentages and thinking, *Why the fuck am I continuing to live like this?*

All my numbers were under 50%. I wasn't happy with anything. Quite frankly, I was miserable.

Some background... I had recently resigned from my day job because I was the subject of workplace bullying. I got abused at work, then came home to be abused by my partner. I was trying to fix this and fix that, change him, change my job, change everything, but I was in a fog of survival and just wasn't thinking clearly at all. I had started my own business after resigning because I was relocating with my partner and my two boys down country to a rural town. I was fairly sure they wouldn't have many opportunities for employment down there, not in my field of expertise anyway, so I bit the bullet and created my little company with the hopes I'd be better off working for myself.

I had zero self-esteem when I met my business coach. In those first few months before I relocated, she helped me get into my head and clear out the shit. The stuff holding me back. We got clear on priorities and we worked on confidence. It was through working with a holistic approach that I recognised my personal life was linked to my professional success.

Within three months of meeting her, I had the strength to leave my abusive relationship, focus on the kids and the relocation (which I couldn't get out of) and go into every day feeling positive and grateful for the little things. I managed to find a part-time job in our new location and got to work building my business. It didn't mean my personal life was any less stressful. I had all sorts of legal things going on in the background and the stress took a toll on my mental health, but the tools I was learning with my unicorn coach helped build my resilience and provide a good attitude to move forward.

I often think maybe I should have left him sooner, or left that job sooner, or started my business sooner, but actually, perhaps I needed to be in the café on that day, at that time with that coach to get the dye your hair purple sooner moment. The stars sort of aligned there. Knowing that my personal and professional success are linked means I have the awareness and the power to make changes that can only affect the business positively. That whole work-life balance thing is complete bollocks these days. I am a single working mother. I flow between personal and professional at least 10 times a day and that's okay.

When I think of my own Legendary Leadership, I think of my children. When I left my abuser, I knew we would be entering a phase that was potentially quite dangerous. I felt very alone in a new town I was unfamiliar with and without much support. I leaned into that. I'm not great with people right off the bat, but I knew my isolation would be a weakness and I refused to be isolated, so I said yes to every meeting, gathering, function, seminar in the hopes to connect with others. Luckily, this was made easier with my part-time job. I introduced my kids to new families from work. I got them into extracurricular activities. I decided, if we were stuck in this new town, we'd become part of the new town. That was hard work, and putting yourself out there is very uncomfortable.

I've been in this town now for five years. I have met some amazing people, my kids have settled, I have some great clients, I'm involved in some challenging and rewarding projects. I have great friends and more support than I ever thought I'd get. I refused to feel alone and I did that by being grateful for what I had, focusing on having a positive attitude, putting myself out there to meet new people and find exciting new opportunities. Maybe I wouldn't have got to where I am now without that Eureka moment in the little French café.

Sarah-Jayne Shine, Graphic Designer, Lemonface Design

A few years ago, I was in that exact position...

I wanted to lose weight. I had undergone a surgery that can sometimes result in weight gain and I had put it off for too long because I didn't want to gain the weight. But then the underlying reasons for needing the surgery began to outweigh the vanity reason for not having it and I ended up being wheeled into theatre. A few months after the surgery, I was feeling amazing apart from one thing... I had gained more weight.

I set about trying to do something about it. Now, before you begin to make your predictions of what happened, let me set the scene for you. I am a facilitator at a monthly retreat for patients of weight loss surgery. During the retreat, I teach and facilitate a number of sessions on mindset and behavioural change so that our patients' surgery can be the best decision they have ever made. The reason I got the gig in the first place? I wrote a book on the psychological blocks to weight loss.

So here I am, fronting up month after month to a new group of patients who are keen to hear what I have to say and find out the silver bullet to successful long-term healthy living, carrying some extra weight. Heck, I have literally written the book on weight loss, and I can't shift my own excess kilos.

Intellectually, I know what I need to be doing, but I cannot translate that into action.

Until...

I began looking at what I wanted to achieve from the lens of my values. You see, I was looking at my goal of losing weight from that place of vanity. I wanted to lose the weight because I didn't like what I saw in the mirror, and the fact that I couldn't wear my cute fifties dresses or find a pair of jeans that fit. But that wasn't important enough to me. I could have looked at the goal to lose weight through the lens of health. Once again, intellectually, I knew the impact on my health to continue to carry the extra kilos, but that wasn't powerful enough for me either.

With values, you cannot outrun what is most important to you, even if you wish it wasn't. And what was and is most important to me is telling the truth and not being fake. I felt like a complete fraud to my audience at the retreat. I felt like I wasn't walking my talk and that I was undermining my own work by saying one thing and doing another. When I began to look at the goal through the lens of being genuine, authentic and honest, everything became easier and the weight came off and stayed off.

We learn our first set of values from our parents or caregivers. They teach us what is most important. It has to be that way, because that's how we learn when we are very young. But how many of us ever question those values that we inherit from our ancestors? And I choose that word "ancestors" carefully, because how often do you think our parents or their parents or their parents ever questioned the values that were instilled in them either? If my experience with my clients is anything to go by, then the answer is not many.

Values shift and change in response to where we are, what we are doing and lots of other factors, but we run into trouble when we believe that our values are one thing when they are actually something else.

TECHNICOLOUR ACTION: WHAT A TECHNICOLOUR LIFE FEELS LIKE

This exercise can give you insight into what your core values are when you think about what's most important to you.

> *When you think about what it looks and feels like to live a life in glorious technicolour, what do you notice?*
>
> *Who do you know is living their life in glorious technicolour and what do you notice about them?*
>
> *What will it feel like to be truly living a bold, genuine, authentic life?*

Living a Technicolour Life is living a life of purpose and impact. You are likely reading this book because you want more of that. What goes into *your* purpose and the impact *you* want to have in the world is your unique blend of core values.

Here are my values for living life in glorious technicolour.

> *Responsibility*
> *Achievement incorporating challenge*
> *Peace*
> *Health*
> *Fun and adventure*
> *Financial security*

Creativity
Purpose
Impact
Honesty and integrity
Ease
Positivity

Let's look at the role that each of these values plays in my Technicolour Life:

I am 100% **responsible** for my results. The actions that I take and the decisions that I make create my outcomes, and no-one but me is responsible for that. This means that I am not in a blame or victim cycle, which is a helpless and hopeless place that would stop me from being 100% me.

I get a huge amount of satisfaction from accomplishment and **achievement**. This means I need to be challenged in order to achieve, but I know that my level of challenge has to be such that I am able to achieve, or else it has the opposite effect. Achievable tasks and goals are key for me. Like writing this book. It's quite a sizeable challenge, but it is absolutely achievable using processes that I will share with you in later chapters. It's all very well to say that you love a challenge, but really knowing how much of a challenge you love will help shape your Technicolour Life.

Peace and stillness are states that I have come to recognise I need in order to fuel my energy. In my twenties, I was a push-through-and-do-it-anyway type of gal, but this left me incredibly depleted and allowed me to keep running in the wrong direction. Peace and stillness is my form of meditation and reflection. It helps to ground me in knowing that I am values-aligned and staying true to myself.

Health is something that is a bit of a challenge for me, but I want to make sure that I am honouring it, because there are still a ton of things I want to do, see and achieve in my Technicolour Life, so it has to be front and centre if I want to accomplish those goals. Doing what I need to do in order to stay healthy isn't always fun, but when I can see that those actions are directly linked to my ability to live my Technicolour Life, it makes it easier to make the right decisions (most of the time!)

Fun and adventure can look like many things. I actually have a ton of fun when I am working or creating. For me, an adventure can be attending a networking event or heading to the speedway. I am still exploring what fun and adventure look like to me. And that is the beauty of this exercise. You get to explore what all of these values look like to you, not some definition in a dictionary, or what they mean to other people.

Financial security affords me the life I lead. I have a long history of struggling with this due to my upbringing, as many people do. It has been hard for me to challenge the beliefs and rules that I made for myself when I was younger and watching my parents struggle through entrepreneurship. This had a huge impact on me growing up. Initially, we lived in a great area in an aspirational home for many, and I grew up believing that we were pretty lucky and well off. I distinctly remember a time when I asked my dad if we were rich. He responded, "We're comfortable." A few years later, after some tough times in my dad's workplace, he left and bought a business and that was the start of decades of money worries for our family. The whole experience caused my dad to become deeply depressed and sometimes take on a victim mentality, which made for incredibly tough times as a family. I made some rules for myself around financial security that I tried to live by for many years. They included never wanting to be my own boss, and never using debt. I'll talk more about the impact of these beliefs later on, because if you are going to live a Technicolour Life, it's important to understand the difference between beliefs and values.

As a recovering engineer, **creativity** is not something that I would have described myself as having, but I realise that I am actually an incredibly creative person—once again, by my own definition. I look at 'traditionally' creative people like storytellers, artists and musicians, and I greatly admire their ability to create beauty from nothing. I am not that kind of creative, but I am creative in that I have a message to share and experiences that others can learn from. I love nothing more than the creative process of curating knowledge to share with my students, or looking at a problem from a different perspective for a client. This is creativity too. It took me a long time to realise and claim my place as a creative person.

Honesty and integrity go hand in hand for me, and allow me to operate from a place of calm. After far too many years of operating in situations and environments that forced me to compromise either or both of these values, this is my absolute necessity in living a life of glorious technicolour. Compromising my honesty and/or integrity is the fastest way for me to end up in the grey. Quite simply, grey areas in honesty and integrity put me in the grey area of life. And I don't like it! For far too long, I thought that the way to 'win' at the game of life was to be dishonest and lack integrity. That was an utterly hopeless place for me. I share these values with my sister, as a result of what we lived through when we were younger. The troubles that my dad went through, and more importantly the way he chose to deal with them, meant that my sister and I spent far more of our formative years keeping secrets and living half-truths for the benefit of what it looked like to outsiders, and it was deeply damaging to me. I am so happy to have realised that I can create a life that allows me to be aligned with these values. I have already shared one story of how powerful these values are to me, and how they helped me to lose weight. It is also what drives my desire for the academy I have created—Coach School—to be the most trusted coach training provider in the world.

Sometimes your values can seem to be at odds with each other. **Ease** and flow is also a value of mine, which on the face of it may appear to be at odds with the idea that my achievements need to have some level of challenge. But the two play different roles and have different purposes. As I alluded to earlier, I need to achieve for sure, but I need to be able to see how I am going to achieve something, or else it seems too hard and I give up before I even begin. Ease and flow also plays into how I love my relationships to work. While I am happy to undertake challenges in my work and career, I prefer when there is more ease and flow in my relationships. Now, being the mother of two teenage daughters, this is not always possible, but defining that value helps me to strive towards it.

Positivity is my rocket fuel. It gets me out of bed in the morning and it keeps me excited about the possibilities of a Technicolour Life. Having watched my dad descend into depression and alcoholism, and developing my own beliefs that compromised my core values, my past contributed to my creating a view of the world that was not positive at all. It made everything hard. Work, relationships, family and friends. Everything felt like I was wading through dark, sticky treacle. When I woke up and began to work on my personal development, I recognised that I could shift my viewpoint to something more positive. It was truly life-changing. Choosing a positive mindset has been a practice that I have spent many years honing. Every moment of effort has been worth it. Positivity helps me to see all the possibilities in front of me and my clients.

When I am aligned to these values, I am living my life on purpose and that is what will allow me to make a positive impact in the world. If you want to be bold, genuine and authentic, you will need to get very familiar with your values, what they mean to you and why.

TECHNICOLOUR ACTION: DEFINE TO ALIGN

Some of your values might be the same as mine, but you will likely have others.

Brainstorm the values that mean the most to you.

Write your definition of what the word means to you.

Here are some values words that might help you to identify yours:

VALUES WORDS

BELONGING	CREATIVITY	GENEROSITY
CONNECTION	RECOGNITION	WISDOM
FRIENDSHIP	JOY	SPIRITUALITY
AFFECTION	LOYALTY	HEALTH
POWER	RESPONSIBILITY	CULTURE
ADVENTURE	FREEDOM	SERENITY
ACHIEVEMENT	WELLBEING	SAFETY
WEALTH	ECONOMIC SECURITY	SELF RESPECT
ENERGY	PLEASURE	INTEGRITY
KNOWLEDGE	COMMUNITY	JUSTICE

VALUES

The combination of values and their definitions should tell you a lot about your purpose and the positive impact that you can be making when you live in glorious technicolour. Explore this further by answering the following questions.

Which would you consider to be your highest value? Explain why.

How do your values show up in your life? (For example, if you value education, you likely will be engaged regularly in study.)

Think back to some past decisions or choices you have made. How did your values show up or not show up?

Who will be attracted to you when you are showing up 100% aligned to those values?

What good can you do in the world when you walk your talk?

Take a moment to reflect on the exercises you have just completed. List any discoveries you have made about yourself.

The Difference Between Values and Beliefs

Beliefs are statements that we choose. We act as if they are true because they fit with our model of the world. Some beliefs are helpful and some are not.

Our values change as we move through our lives in response to our life experiences. However, while beliefs can be changed to better support our values, our values cannot be easily changed to support our beliefs.

In the previous section, I shared that I developed some beliefs in response to what was going on as I was growing up. As I got older, I was often told that I was like my dad. Family members would tell me how much I looked like him, how much my sense of humour was like him and how my mannerisms were like him. This is all well and good for a time. It gave me a real sense of belonging and fitting in. I loved being like my dad. After all, a young girl's dad is her superhero, right? Until he's not.

It was desperately difficult for me to watch my dad struggle with finances, depression, relationships and alcohol all while believing that I was so like him. The phrase that went through my head often was 'history repeats itself'. I was terrified of making the same choices as my dad. I was petrified that I was going to follow his path, even if I did everything differently. Because the narrative remained "you're so like your dad."

I tried to run away. I moved to London after university, in part, to try to be myself. But it didn't take long for me to run into debt on my rent and living expenses, which was evidence that I wasn't good with finances and therefore "just like my dad".

This is just one instance of a belief narrative that I was running. I had a whole host of them.

"I'm not loveable."
"I'll never be popular."
"I'm ugly."
"I'm a fraud."
"If I'm nice then people won't see through me."
"People are generally out to get one over on me."
"Life is a battle and a struggle."
"You'll never fit in."

Maybe you hear your own inner critic say some of the same things?

My inner critic was super strong because I listened to her to the exclusion of everything and everyone else. The thing is that your inner critic has a captive audience and usually says things that no-one would say out loud. It's right there feeding this BS into you over and over. I kept running and it took me a long time to realise I could change my course. It was long after I began living my life my way that those beliefs shifted. In fact, that is the main driver of why I do the work I do now. It's why I wrote this book. It's why I run my programs. It's why I work 1:1 with clients in my coaching practice. I want to drastically shorten this process for others so that they don't have to wait as long as I did for those beliefs to change.

That being said, I can only want it for you as much as you want it for yourself. (That's why it is so important for you to complete the exercises in this book or reach out for more help if you need it.)

Change doesn't come from just thinking about it. Change comes from behaviour, especially behaviour that others can't see, like beating yourself up.

Limiting Beliefs

Beliefs start as statements, just like the statements that my family and extended family were saying to me about being like my dad. No-one said these things with any knowledge or intention of them becoming damaging. They were just making a seemingly innocuous observation. However, when you hear that same observation over and over, it begins to stick. If beliefs are created in times of our lives when we don't feel safe, instead of being true and helpful, we might call them 'limiting beliefs'. We are not always aware of these beliefs as they exist in our subconscious mind, yet they influence the majority of what we do, think and feel.

The job of limiting beliefs is to keep us safe from experiencing physical or emotional pain. It's as if someone else was giving us advice or a warning to protect us. However, these beliefs can mean we stay stuck where we are or 'blocked'. Instead of moving forward and trusting our ability to learn from experiences, we believe something that isn't true. Sometimes we need to dive beneath the surface to better understand what is going on.

Above the Surface
Behaviours—how I act and what is seen
Self-talk—what I say to myself

Below the Surface
Emotions—what I am feeling
Beliefs—what I believe to keep me safe

TECHNICOLOUR TOOL: SEEING YOUR SELF-TALK

Complete this exercise now for different aspects of your life:

When I am at work:

Behaviour—how do I act and what do others see?	Self-talk—what do I say to myself?
Emotions—how am I really feeling?	Beliefs—what do I believe that keeps me safe?

When I am at home:

Behaviour—how do I act and what do others see?	Self-talk—what do I say to myself?
Emotions—how am I really feeling?	Beliefs—what do I believe that keeps me safe?

When I am with friends:

Behaviour—how do I act and what do others see?	Self-talk—what do I say to myself?
Emotions—how am I really feeling?	Beliefs—what do I believe that keeps me safe?

Deconstructing or challenging limiting beliefs can be a relatively straightforward process. The real art is identifying the belief in play. Often you won't be aware of it. You'll just know that something keeps getting in the way of what you are trying to do or achieve.

The three main limiting beliefs that I see time and again are:

"I am not enough"
"I am not worthy or deserving"
"I am not loveable"

You can see that "I am not enough" really covers all three. Most of my clients have a sense of not being enough in at least one aspect of their life.

A note on positive beliefs: Positive beliefs can be as damaging as negative beliefs. The labels that we are given as children can be damaging even if they seem encouraging on the face of it. For example, the label "you're so smart" can be just as damaging as one that implies the opposite. This might be something that you are familiar with, being the achiever that you are.

What happens to the girl who has been told that she's so smart all through childhood?

What happens when school starts to get tougher?

What happens when she has the label of being the 'smart one' and believes she has to live up to it?

When things get even harder at university, at work, or in relationships, but this belief has become an identity, what does it say about her now?

Something as simple as a positive statement reinforced over and over has now stifled her. Her identity is at risk of being dismantled because she hasn't been given the opportunity to fail and then figure out the solution. It is in being allowed to fail and knowing we will survive that resilience is built. When we don't give our children, colleagues or friends credit for what they have done to achieve their successes and merely comment on the outcomes or the perceived traits, we are setting them up for a fall down the line.

Limiting beliefs are often buried deep beneath the surface and it can be tricky to identify our own limiting beliefs, but there are some behaviours and language patterns that can indicate that a limiting belief may be lurking.

Behaviour indicators are anything that you are doing that takes you further away, rather than towards your goal or vision. For example, if you want to lose 10 kgs, but keep eating the wrong foods, or you want to make videos for your business, but find every reason under the sun not to get in front of the camera, or maybe you want to go for a promotion, but you avoid asking for recommendations on LinkedIn.

We can also find evidence of limiting beliefs through the **language** that you use to yourself and to others. The language that we use in everyday life both represents and impacts how we experience our world. We attempt to capture thoughts, ideas and to describe what we see around us using words. Inevitably things get 'lost in translation'. This is referred to as distortion. Distortion is where some aspects of ideas and experiences are given more weight and focus that others. We all do this both consciously and subconsciously. And the way we distort points to our underlying beliefs about ourselves, others and the world.

Here are the most common language-based distortions that I see, and how to challenge them if you find yourself using them:

All-or-nothing thinking

Seeing things as right or wrong with nothing in between. All-or-nothing thinking sounds like:

- "I didn't finish writing that book so it was a complete waste of time."
- "There's no point in applying for that speaking opportunity if I'm not an expert."
- "They didn't show. They're completely unreliable!"

Challenging all-or-nothing thinking can be as simple as asking yourself, "What else might be going on here?" or "What is another option?"

Overgeneralisation

Overgeneralisation is a term for using words like "always" or "never" in relation to a single event or experience. It's very common and sounds like:

- "I'll ***never*** get that promotion."
- "She's ***always*** late."

The way to deal with overgeneralisation is to find an exception to the always or never rule. For example, is she really always late or has there ever been a time when she was on time?

Minimising, magnifying or catastrophising

This is when we see things as dramatically more or less important than they actually are. If you have ever been called a 'drama queen', this might be what was going on!

This is when we make up catastrophic endings to stories that leave us feeling further away from what we are trying to achieve. An example from a weight loss client might be that they 'cheat' on their food plan and the thought pattern that follows tells them they will always be overweight and no-one will ever love them and they would be better off being alone.

The solution to this distortion is once again to look for another possible outcome.

Summary

Discovery is hard work, but it is also incredibly worthwhile. Most people resist self-examination and this keeps them living their life in grayscale. They are in such a rush to get to the next thing and the next thing and the next that they miss out on laying the solid foundations that can be built on forever.

Discovery is the longest section of this book and for good reason. This stage is not about the 'how', so try not to concern yourself with that right now. If you are feeling the pull to race ahead and see what comes next, know that it is perfectly natural, but to get the best from the time you are spending with this book, I encourage you to give yourself the space to complete this self-discovery chapter as fully as you can. It will help you to get the best from the rest of the book.

Discovery takes time, Commitment and courage. There will be parts of this chapter that you have been able to complete as you moved through, and other parts that you might have found more challenging and chosen to skip over for now. The tools and exercises in this chapter are not 'one and done'. The constant refining of the work laid out in this chapter is lifelong and I invite you to go back over the exercises you did complete or have your first attempt at the ones you did not.

Clients are often surprised how long they spend in Discovery, but it really is the launch-pad for their future success. The more self-discovery you do, the more Clarity you will gain. It does take Courage to dig deep and question the parts of ourselves that we might not be so proud of, but it is the first step to truly understanding ourselves which leads to showing up in a Consistent way.

CHAPTER TWO

Align

"Just as your car runs more smoothly and requires less energy to go faster and farther when the wheels are in perfect alignment, you perform better when your thoughts, feelings, emotions, goals and values are in balance"

~Brian Tracy

I am about to show my age here. Okay, let's just rip the band-aid off. At the time of writing, I am 46 years old. That means that I grew up in a pre-internet era, in the time of vinyl records and cassette recorders. It was before mobile phones, let alone smartphones. It was before streaming services like Netflix and Disney+. In fact, growing up, we only had three TV channels to choose from!

In those days, in order to listen to music or the latest sports scores, we used to have to tune the radio stations. That meant physically turning a dial on the radio receiver to find the station we wanted to hear. You had to tune your radio into that specific frequency by turning a knob to find a specific channel. Most radio stations would incorporate their tuning frequency into their station name or jingle. I grew up listening to Radio Clyde 102.5 FM. Where I live now there is a radio station called Beach FM 106.3.

In between channels, there was interference and white noise. If you didn't tune your radio just right, you would pick up that interference, white noise or even music from another channel. But when you tuned your radio just right, the sound was crystal clear and everything came into clear, sharp focus.

This is what it's like when you are living in a way that is aligned to your beliefs, values and goals. This is how it feels when what you are Doing perfectly matches how you are Being.

It is unrealistic to expect to be able to align all of the personal discovery work that you have just begun to your life in one day. Like everything that is worthwhile, it all takes time and a level of commitment. Trust me, it is worth it though. If you are stuck on something that you have been trying to achieve or change for a long time, I would wager that you will see yourself in this chapter.

Lots of people are unaligned because alignment is hard. There is a perception that it's easy but it's not. This is where Courage comes in: courage to go against the grain, courage to not fit in, courage to be yourself.

Being and Doing

There is much talk about being in your Zone of Genius and Zone of Excellence thanks to Gay Hendricks' excellent book *The Big Leap*. I like to think of it as your Zone of Technicolour: the intersection or overlap of what you are Doing and how you are Being in order to live your Technicolour Life.

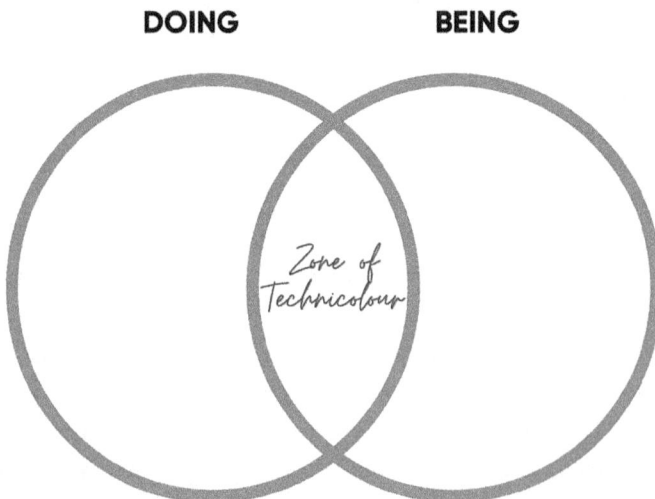

DOING   BEING

Zone of Technicolour

This can look different in each area of your life.

For example, when you are at work, what are you Doing?

Here's what this might look like for me:

What I am Doing	How I am Being
Admin	Distracted
Bookkeeping	Challenged and frustrated
Writing	Inspired
Coaching	Present
Teaching	Confident
Speaking	Nervous and excited
Pitching	Nervous
Creating content	Sometimes inspired, sometimes struggling
Planning	Sometimes overwhelmed, sometimes clear

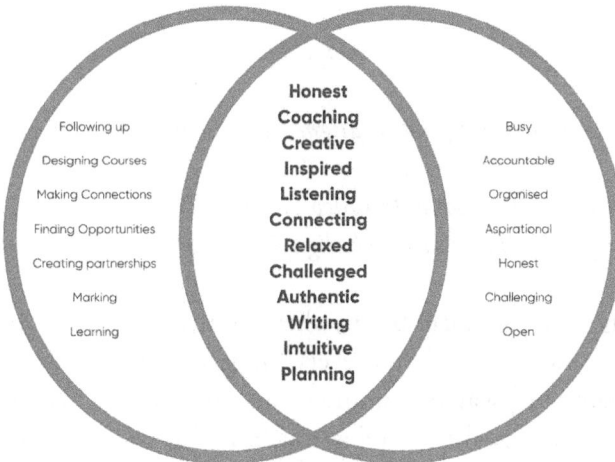

From this, you can clearly see when I am operating in my Zone of Technicolour and when I need to outsource the activities that take me out of it.

TECHNICOLOUR ACTION: GETTING IN THE ZONE

Thinking about your work, what are all the things you are Doing and how are you Being?

Where is the intersection of those things?

What work falls into your Zone of Technicolour?

Thinking about your personal life, what are all the things you are Doing and how are you Being?

Where is the intersection of those things?

What personal life elements are in your Zone of Technicolour?

Where is there crossover between your work and personal Zones of Technicolour?

What are you doing that is not aligned with your values?

What are you doing that is aligned with your values?

Looking back to your Technicolour Life Wheel, do the areas where you are more satisfied align more with your values?

Your perfectly tuned spot can be anywhere on the continuum, but be aware that there is a sweet spot where everything is truly aligned and you are Being and Doing in a way that improves all parts of your Technicolour Life Wheel. Make it your goal to spend as much time as you can in your Zone of Technicolour and remove as many of the other Being and Doing activities as you can.

Fear and Courage

"Your fear will always be triggered by your creativity, because creativity asks you to enter into realms of uncertain outcome, and fear hates uncertain outcome."

~Elizabeth Gilbert, *Big Magic*

We're going to have to talk about the F-word.

Fear.

Fear and the actions that you take when your fear centre is triggered (called self-sabotage) are what stand in the way of being aligned to living life the way you Discovered you want to in the previous chapter.

There are two types of fear: conscious and subconscious. **Conscious fear** is when you are afraid of something and you are aware of that something. It's something like standing on the edge of the bungee jump and wondering why the heck you thought this was a good idea. **Subconscious fear** is fear at a much deeper level that you are not even aware is there.

The definition of **courage** is to do something that frightens you. And right now living in technicolour might be that thing. If it wasn't, you probably wouldn't be reading this book, right?

In 2008, I moved my family across the world from Scotland to New Zealand. We chose New Zealand specifically because my husband didn't have family there. He comes from a large family who are spread out across the world. Our rationale was that if we were going to make this change, then we might as well go all-in and really see if we could make a life for our two young daughters on our own.

From the time we started to make it public that we were planning to make the move, until even now when people ask why I moved halfway round the world, I would get the same response…

"You're so brave."

Usually quickly followed by, "I could never do that."

Yet, I've never considered myself to be brave, and certainly not for following the process that took me from where I was unhappy to where I was happy. (Don't get me wrong, there are some downsides to leaving your friends and family behind, namely leaving your friends and family behind!) To me, it would have taken more effort on my part to stay where I was, knowing I wasn't happy, always wondering what might have been. In truth, staying there frightened me and leaving it behind felt like running away.

How does this relate to fear and its inner workings, though? Fear gets a terribly bad rap in my opinion. It has been cast as the bad guy for far too long and that needs to stop. Fear is not something to be avoided; it is something to be understood.

By asking you to live your life 100% as yourself, I am advocating for a life of creativity. It may not be creativity in its traditional sense, but now that you are the architect of your own path, you will likely be feeling the same emotions as writers, artists, musicians and other creatives. From now on, see yourself as the creator of your life in technicolour. You are the Legendary Leader of your own bold, authentic life and Legendary Leaders are pioneers. They do things that no-one has done before. They live their life from a place of curiosity…

And curiosity is the antidote to fear.

> *"Dearest Fear: Creativity and I are about to go on a road trip together. I understand you'll be joining us, because you always do. I acknowledge that you believe you have an important job to do in my life, and that you take your job seriously. Apparently your job is to induce complete panic whenever I'm about to do anything interesting—and, may I say, you are superb at your job. So by all means, keep doing your job, if you feel you must. But I will also be doing my job on this road trip, which is to work hard and stay focused. And Creativity will be doing its job, which is to remain stimulating and inspiring. There's plenty of room in this vehicle for all of us, so make yourself at home, but understand this: Creativity and I are the only ones driving."*
>
> ~Elizabeth Gilbert, *Big Magic*

This quote from my favourite author on fear, Elizabeth Gilbert, teaches us that fear is not to be feared. Fear has a very important job to do. Fear keeps us safe. But sometimes, if we give it too much free rein, it can hold us back from doing what we really want to do.

I grew up in a time and place where it was not the done thing to *feel*. I am from Glasgow in Scotland, which is known as being a tough town. Now let's be clear, I came from a very nice (some might say posh) part of Glasgow, but there is something in the psyche of all Glaswegians that toughens us. We are not supposed to show weakness, which gets interpreted as we are not supposed to show any emotion. To a degree, this is not specific to Glasgow, or even the UK, but actually prevalent across many parts of the world and has been for generations.

To understand the art of avoidance we need to look deeper into how we are taught to manage emotions from an early age.

Emotions are just a physiological response to some sort of stimulus or trigger. There has to be some sort of indication that tells us to start feeling a certain way. If we think about being happy, then there has to be a message to tell us to start getting happy. After all, we may be content or satisfied, but we are not joyfully happy all of the time. Something happens that triggers the message to start getting happy and the feelings that we associate with happiness start to build as a result. They build and build until they begin to level off and then dissipate. After all, if they just continued to grow exponentially, we'd never get anything done! The intensity of the feeling and how long we feel it for will change in response to the situation, but generally this is the curve that our feelings will take if left to their own devices.

And that is important, because for the most part we leave so-called "positive emotions" like happiness, excitement, joy, satisfaction, serenity to their own devices. It's so-called "negative emotions" that we start to mess with and that is where the problem lies.

Imagine the same scenario as above. Something has to happen to send us the message to start feeling that negative emotion of fear, sadness, anger, guilt and so on. Once we receive the message, those feelings start to build. But when we begin to notice them, what happens? We avoid them! We do anything we can to distract ourselves from that feeling. In fact, when we begin to try and avoid the negative emotion, we can embark on behaviours that seriously sabotage our success.

This is what our parents and caregivers taught us when we were growing up...

"Don't feel sad."

"Don't feel angry."

"Don't be scared."

This came from a loving place, because the people who taught us the art of avoidance probably thought they were doing it in our best interests. From a deeply caring place, they taught us to run away as soon as we noticed those feelings build. However, what that did was rob us of the deep knowing that we can survive the discomfort produced by those feelings.

It's a lot like the 'just do it', 'do it anyway' and 'push through' messages that I mentioned earlier. We are being taught—not just by our family, but by society—not to feel but to push down those emotions that are not deemed acceptable and just get on with it. In my experience with hundreds of clients, taking that approach doesn't work forever. At some point, we all realise that we just can't keep going like that. Eventually, we hit that brick wall and simply don't have the energy to push through anymore.

Existing like this is dangerous. It leads to burnout, depression and feelings of hopelessness. All from not being 'allowed' to feel perfectly natural feelings and learn how to manage them in a healthy way.

As I have mentioned, before becoming an executive coach and speaker, I was a radio frequency engineer, first in Scotland where I was raised, and then in New Zealand where I've lived for over a decade. At the peak of that engineering career, I was leading my team so effectively that the whole office culture was modelled on us. Now, nothing was *wrong* with my engineering career exactly. I wasn't unhappy, but I didn't feel I was being 100% myself either. I was going through the motions at my day job to keep that steady salary while running my executive coaching business on the side and dreaming of creating my own coaching certification.

Of course, there were all sorts of challenges, some that I relished more than others, but one of the biggest came a few years ago when I had to make a choice between my job and my parents.

One day, my parents announced they were travelling all the way from Scotland to come visit for six weeks. The timing was fixed because my mum wanted to spend her 70th birthday with me and my children, her only grandchildren. The problem? I didn't have any annual leave left.

After exploring as many options as I could—such as applying for leave without pay, which was rejected, trying to find flexible working hours or work-from-home options, which were also rejected, and gently enquiring as to whether my parents might come another time, which my mum could not to be encouraged to do—I had to choose whether to:

- Quit the job I'd worked so hard for, trust that I could provide for my family with just my coaching business income, and redefine what success looked like for me; or
- Miss an incredibly rare opportunity to spend quality time with my parents, and as it turned out, the last opportunity I would ever get to do that.

You can probably guess which one I chose. And while it was heart-wrenching to leave a job I was great at, and while I was scared to be 100% me in my coaching business, it was the first time I really became the leader of myself, my life, and my true desires, not just the leader my career expected me to be.

I knew in my heart it was the right thing to do, but I was terrified of the unknown. I was scared that my decision was selfish and that my family might live to regret it. It brought back all the feelings I'd had when my dad had gone into business and how that had turned out for him. Even with all the work I had done, those creeping fears of history repeating itself came back. I felt torn in two.

Yet, my gut was telling me it was the right decision.

The night after I resigned I sat in my kitchen and sobbed. For probably the first time in my life, I allowed myself to *just feel* without any attempt to stem the flow of tears. I didn't try to come up with an answer, or a solution, or a fix. I just allowed myself to be sad and scared and to cry it out.

That experience taught me that I could survive those feelings of fear and sadness. And if I can do it once, I can damn well do it again. It was a pivotal moment in so many ways. And, as it turned out, it *was* the right decision on so many levels. Not least because it was the last time I saw my dad.

You see, negative feelings follow the same curve as positive feelings. They build and then they dissipate. In the survival of that curve, we learn courage. In the survival of that curve, we learn that fear is not to be feared. In the survival of that curve, we build resilience which fuels us to try more courageous actions that are values-aligned and technicoloured.

DYE YOUR HAIR PURPLE SOONER MOMENT: SANDY

Looking back, I feel that everything has happened very organically for me. I always took chances and put myself out there even if it scared the heck out of me.

One of the scariest times, but with the biggest reward, was giving a keynote speech to a graduating college class. I actually was supposed to be there to talk about trends but the keynote speaker suddenly couldn't make it. At the time, I had never spoken to a large group. It was always something I avoided. I saw myself as a behind-the-scenes kind of gal. After the presentation, I had a line waiting to speak to me and I was offered a job as an adjunct professor, went on to win two awards and wrote the curriculum for the college. Most importantly, it gave me the courage to host fashion shows and appear on TV.

After having children, the job market was a bit scarce. I heard about a fashion editor's position, got a phone interview with the editor-in-chief that led to a second interview with her. But before she hung up the phone, she said (in a very Devil Wears Prada kind of way), "Be prepared if you get this job. You will have very big shoes to fill." It was terrifying. I had stayed home for years and didn't really feel qualified.

I went to her office for the interview anyway. I had the two-page spread already done and added a presentation. I went on to write two columns over a 10-year period.

Stepping into your fear brings the biggest rewards. Without trying, I wouldn't have realised how much I had to share or how many people I could help.

Sandy Hapoienu, personal branding stylist

Next time you experience something that makes you feel sad, angry, frustrated, or any other 'negative' emotion, give yourself the time and grace to sit with it curiously. Just sit and notice the feeling as it builds. Resist the temptation to fix or avoid the feeling; that is not the purpose of the exercise.

The purpose is to notice the curve and recognise that it is safe to sit in those feelings without attachment to the outcome. When you have done it once, you might find that the next time it is not so intense, or that the feeling doesn't last as long.

How to Stay Grey (AKA Self-Sabotage)

My definition of self-sabotage is doing things that don't make sense. It's knowing intellectually that you want something, but subconsciously getting in your own way by doing things that take you further away from what you desire, namely living your Technicolour Life.

I mentioned earlier that there is conscious fear and subconscious fear. Self-sabotaging behaviour comes from subconscious fear. This can be tricky because you could be doing everything technically 'right' in order to bring your life into alignment, but something just seems to be getting in the way and you can't quite figure out why. An example of this would be deciding that you want to drop a few kilos and knowing intellectually what you need to do, but not being able to resist the sweet treats that keep you above your goal weight. In some cases it can look like doing all the right things all week, then having an unexpected argument with your partner. Before you know it, you've raided the cupboard or fridge and polished off a packet of biscuits or a bottle of wine. It happened so fast, you weren't even aware of what you were doing.

Another example is wanting a promotion, but finding every reason under the sun not to update your CV.

There are a number of ways that self-sabotage commonly presents itself. As you have already seen in the limiting beliefs section, these behaviours are often subconscious. For the remainder of this book, you will examine and begin the practice of resolving your self-sabotage behaviours.

Let's start with the most common self-sabotage behaviours that I see in my clients:

- *Being late*
- *Overeating, consuming too much alcohol*
- *Starting an argument with a colleague or loved one*
- *Turning down opportunities*
- *Accepting opportunities that cannot be fulfilled*

- *Postponing things like events or launching a business or product*
- *Procrastinating*
- *Waiting until everything is perfect*

These ring immediate alarm bells that fear is at work.

You might see yourself in some of the behaviours above. It's outside the scope of this book to delve into every one of them, but if I have done my job right and put this book into the hands of those who I intended it for, then you will identify with perfectionism and/or procrastination, so we will dive deeper into those.

Perfectionism and procrastination are two sides of the same coin as far as I am concerned.

Perfectionism

Perfectionism is an excuse wrapped up in a pretty bow. Perfectionism is doing your best, but still never feeling like it's good enough. Perfectionism is fear of scrutiny plain and simple.

If you are waiting for everything to be perfect you are holding yourself back from being in alignment. Alignment needs movement and iteration and growth, but perfectionism holds you back from that movement and flow. Not putting out that piece of work, that piece of art, that website, that book, that song—wherever you are holding back because you think it's not good enough yet and you're still working on it, that is perfectionism. And it makes sense, but there's a fine line. We have been brought up as good girls to do our best, to not be sloppy, to demonstrate how smart or talented we are.

But at what cost?

Living a bold, genuine, authentic life means that you need to experiment. You need to test the theories of what will actually happen if you put yourself and your ideas, opinions and work out into the world.

Most of my clients identify with the idea of perfectionism and struggle with even constructive criticism—although they often tell themselves that they don't.

I get it. I really do. While writing this book, I delivered a keynote presentation on Legendary Leadership for an international women's conference. I was trying out some new material and had agreed with my coach that this particular event wasn't too big a risk for me profile-wise. It was a calculated risk. The very point of me doing the event was experimentation. I showed up, took the stage and I ran out of time! When I say I ran out of time, I mean I ran out of time with a whole section of my presentation not covered. I covered off my main content, but the summary piece that brought everything together and demonstrated how my teaching points sat within my body of work was missing.

This was not even my first presentation and I had practiced multiple times before the event. I was gutted, embarrassed and shocked that I had misread this so badly. If I was at the beginning of my speaking or teaching career, then fair enough, but I would consider myself a fairly experienced amateur.

Even as the MC was thanking me for my "very comprehensive and fact-filled presentation", I was telling myself how badly I had failed, how I had put far too much into the presentation "like I always do" and how I had let myself, the organiser and the audience down. Even with the knowledge that my goal for the presentation was to experiment with this new material and new ways of delivering it, even with gathering great information and data about how I can simplify and improve for the next event, and even when my presenter feedback came through in an email a few days later saying I scored 4.2 out of 5, I felt ashamed knowing I had not done my best.

So, when I say that I know how it feels to be a perfectionist, please trust that we are speaking from one to another.

And it makes sense, right? The conditioning that we have as children, particularly as girls and then women, is to be perfect. To look perfect, to sound perfect, to achieve, to be graceful, to be gracious, to be fucking perfect. It's no wonder that we revert back to wanting or needing to be perfect once we are successful by external standards, but want to be successful in our own right by being 100% ourselves. But seeking to be perfect is just avoidance of the fear of being *seen* as something less than or not good enough.

The great thing about living a Technicolour Life is that *you* get to decide what is good enough. I may have had a few moments of reverting back to feeling not good enough after that last presentation, but I haven't let those moments stop me. I didn't let perfectionism stop me from getting on that stage in the first place.

That would not have been true without the work I've done, the work that I am sharing here and that you are doing in this book. Now I don't get bogged down in the mire of criticising myself or let the feeling of not being ready stop me from taking an opportunity, but it has taken time to get to this point.

A powerful reframe that really helped me to get here was to treat everything as an experiment. Whenever I try something new and scary, I remind myself that I wouldn't expect anyone else to get things perfect the first time, so why would I hold myself to that impossible standard? Remember there is no failure, only feedback. With every attempt, we create information, data, evidence that we can use to shape what we need to tweak or optimise the *next time*. And I think that is an important point to make too. When I began to look at opportunities that scared me a little from the perspective of *this is the first time* I am doing this, rather than *this is the only time* I am doing this, it gave me space to be a little bit kinder to myself. And with every attempt, I create more data and more evidence that I am taking imperfect action in the right direction. By committing to practice, I can now recognise the difference between being brave enough to try something out, and not even being in the running.

There are two pieces of inspiration that have significantly helped me to get to this point. One is from Brené Brown's *Daring Greatly*. The quote is not from Brown herself, but Teddy Roosevelt in a 1910 address.

> *"It is not the critic who counts; not the man who points out how the strong man stumbles, or where the doer of deeds could have done them better. The credit belongs to the man who is actually in the arena, whose face is marred by dust and sweat and blood; who strives valiantly; who errs, who comes short again and again, because there is no effort without error and shortcoming; but who does actually strive to do the deeds; who knows great enthusiasms, the great devotions; who spends himself in a worthy cause; who at the best knows in the end the triumph of high achievement, and who at the worst, if he fails, at least fails while daring greatly."*
>
> ~Theodore Roosevelt

When I began to question some of my perfectionist behaviour and really shift it, I realised that I was surrounded by people who were not in my arena. They were on the side-lines telling me what to do. Worse! They were telling me what I *should* do. But the fact was that they had no idea what I should do, because they weren't doing it! These were people I deeply loved, admired and trusted, and I was holding myself back because I didn't want to let them down. But then I had this greater realisation that they didn't have a clue about what I was doing because they had not been there themselves.

It was then that I began to pay a whole lot less attention to the talkers in my life. I still love, respect, admire and trust them, but they are not doers. They will think themselves into analysis paralysis and never take action. (If you recognise yourself in that last statement, stay tuned!) Now I only act on the advice of people who are in the arena getting their asses kicked and eating dirt just like me. Those are the people who have something I want to hear.

The second piece of inspirational advice that shattered my perfectionism glass ceiling was in an interview between two of my favourite online business mentors Denise Duffield-Thomas (author and money-mindset mentor) and Natalie MacNeil (Emmy-award-winning media entrepreneur, four times best-selling author and business mentor). Denise said that she had given herself permission to *contribute* to the conversation of money mindset. She hadn't set out to be the expert or the only one who could talk about it. She recognised she was *contributing*. At that time, that is exactly what I needed to hear, and I hope that it is powerful for you too.

We can all contribute to the world that we want to create and take part in. It takes way more than one expert to change the world. Contribute to the conversations that you are interested in. Stimulate discussion and get curious. Ask questions and don't expect to have all the answers. Commit to learning. You can still inspire and teach others as you go.

Leading by example and living your bold, authentic, genuine Technicolour Life is never done. Give yourself permission to start wherever you are right now, because you learn by doing.

Procrastination and Analysis Paralysis

Let's take a look at what's going on with procrastination, or as some of my clients describe it, laziness. This belief of being lazy is an indicator to me that someone is not in alignment because often they are some of the busiest people you'll meet. It's just that there are some things they can't seem to get around to doing, but I know that there is a reason for that, and it is certainly not laziness.

Let me explain what I mean.

It really hurts my heart when my clients and students describe themselves as lazy, because I know that they are not. They are more than willing to put in the hard yards to achieve something that they want, and they have put in many, many hours to get to where they are now. Lazy is not the problem. It's knowing how to motivate yourself. This is something that we'll talk about more later in the book, but for now let's take a look at procrastination.

Procrastination and perfectionism go hand in hand because they are, in effect, the same thing. Where perfectionism is the fear of scrutiny, procrastination is the fear of knowing where to start. Procrastinators aren't lazy; they're overwhelmed.

To understand this fully, we need to take a look into the different aspects of our brain. Now don't get scared. This is not a brain science lesson. I am ill-qualified for that! However, it is important to have an appreciation of what's at play here so that you can learn to work with it, rather than rail against it and then call yourself nasty names like lazy, dumb or stupid.

I like to think of the brain as having three "layers":

Layer 1—the thinking brain, or Head Brain

This layer is pretty much our conscious mind. It's where we do all our thinking. It's where we weigh up pros and cons, keep our to-do lists and analyse everything. This is the most recent part of our brain to have developed in an evolutionary sense, and it's also the last part of our brains to develop as we grow into adults.

Layer 2—the feeling brain, or Heart Brain

This layer is where our emotions, memories and feelings live. It's all about the feels. This layer forms part of your subconscious mind.

Layer 3—the instinctive brain, or Gut Brain

This layer is the most ancient part of our brain. It's responsible for all things survival. It regulates temperature, makes sure we breathe when we sleep and keeps our heart beating. It is also where our fear centre lives and it is responsible for our fight-flight-freeze instinct. This is the other part of our subconscious mind.

While our thinking brain can cope with all sorts of complex concepts and ideas, the instinctive brain is still stuck in ancient times looking out for threats to survival. And here's the rub. It's the instinctive brain who is still running the show. When you actually look at the pathways to each layer, the shortest pathway is to the instinctive brain, then through the limbic layer before eventually reaching the thinking brain. What that means is it doesn't really matter what you think consciously, because your instinctive brain is going to be making decisions for you before you are even aware.

For the purposes of the instinctive brain, this is what we want, right? We want it to take charge if our survival is under threat and just do what needs to be done to get us out of danger. We really don't need to have a committee meeting about it. If there is a bear coming at me, I don't want to be coming up with the pros and cons of my options. I want to get out of there as quickly as I can.

But when was the last time you came up against a bear?

Our instinctive brain has not moved with the times. It's still there doing its job, but without the finesse that modern-day living perhaps requires. We don't really need to have the same response to a goal, project or idea as we would have to a threat to our survival, but that is what is happening.

While perfectionism is your flight or avoidance response, you can think of procrastination as your freeze response. When a client tells me that they are struggling with procrastination or analysis paralysis, that tells me they are trying to do something that is too big. The result is that your instinctive brain comes in to save you and you end up in freeze mode.

DYE YOUR HAIR PURPLE SOONER MOMENT: PAM

I don't know when our sense of fear kicks in, nor when we develop the ability to question everything that might happen as we try to make the big decisions that are not so scary, but seem so scary, but fear can be crippling, even for the small decisions. Of course, these things must start in our childhood as we are taught to be "good" and not rock the boat. Later, we're told to pick a career that is "safe" and then we might take a "secure" job in a large corporate where there are many standards and norms. Those things all exist for a reason, and companies do want people to thrive, but there are also very clear unwritten corporate cultures about what is acceptable and what is not acceptable—some of which have been around for hundreds of years. Having worked in a large, multinational for so long, perhaps my success there was the result of my fear to not step outside of those norms.

I left that "big" corporate career about four years ago. For 25 years, I worked hard, got paid and did all the right things. It was comfortable, I worked with good people and we worked on good projects. While it was a big step into the unknown, I was leaving to start my own company and focus on supporting people with diabetes. Several years before I left, when my son was just 20 months old, he was diagnosed with Type 1 diabetes. At the time, there was no real support where we lived. I knew that had to change.

One thing I always dreamed about was creating a community and a space where children like my son and their parents who were in the same position as me could meet and support each other as they navigated their way through this irreversible autoimmune condition. This included plans for an event to bring the community together. Not just one event, but several events in different forms. This was something I wanted to see happen so badly as I felt it could help a lot of people, but I did not move on this idea for several years.

In a new company, there are of course many hats to wear and things to do. As an entrepreneur, building a start-up, the list is endless. Despite having organised international corporate events for hundreds of people, I was not able to step into my grass-roots movement to launch my company's own small event for something that was so near and dear to my heart.

When I finally decided to do it, I started planning for an event in the spring of 2020. Things were busy, but I told myself, "Enough already". It was time. As things started to come together, I was honestly shocked. I realised that the reasons I had not executed my plans for an event before was because I didn't think that the companies who stepped up to sponsor the event would really care or want to participate. I was afraid that people would not register. I kept worrying about what people would think. Or worse, no-one showing up. Some companies who work in this space told me, "Don't feel bad if only four people show up. It happens." But much to my surprise, none of those things happened. The response was overwhelming.

After waiting for so long, due to the wonderful support from both the business community and the charity to which all registration fees would be donated, I decided that if only four people showed up, then I would show up for those four people. If I did not fully show up, open-heartedly and unconditionally, no-one else would. Of course, I hoped for more than four people, but at that moment, I was truly ready to give four people just as much of myself as four hundred people.

As we were planning the event, we started hearing about this virus in other parts of the world. We kept reading the news that the numbers were growing, and some experts were raising their eyebrows. There were whispers wondering if large conferences and events would be cancelled. I started getting messages from concerned parents wondering if we would continue.

Then it happened. Many large-scale events started voluntarily cancelling. This was truly devastating as it was peak season for them. One of my sponsors even pulled a diabetes ambassador from my event because they felt it might be unsafe to travel. Yes, people cared that much that I had some very special guests who were going to attend from abroad to meet the children and families in my community. It was so heart-warming.

With no clear statement from the authorities yet, we kept our hopes up and continued planning. But as more events cancelled, it became obvious. I made the decision to cancel. Then two days later, the announcement came. Schools would be closed and all events were off. That was it.

I admit I felt relieved, because there was no more uncertainty. I would no longer wonder if cancelling was the right thing to do. Now, several months into it, we know that it was absolutely the right thing to do.

Back then, though, as I wrote a personal email to each sponsor and those who registered, I just kept shaking my head. I *could not* believe that I had waited so long. I was finally doing it. Then BAM!

Just like that, COVID-19 had other plans.

Three months later, even though things are opening slowly and face masks are mandatory, it is not clear when it will be safe to schedule this event. I am in no hurry as I want everyone to feel good and be safe.

But lesson learned—do not wait. Why was I waiting? It was such a small decision in the grand scheme of things, but for some reason that fear of being seen held me back from doing it in previous years. It's so odd because the event doesn't even have anything to do with me being seen. I wouldn't care if I was seen, or got the credit for it. My reward would come from seeing so many smiling faces leaving the event feeling inspired and a little bit better about having a chronic condition that they never asked for.

Realising this has made me a lot more fearless in how I run my business, the business decisions that I make, and life in general. For one, I do not over-study the risks of doing something as much as I used to. I mean, I am still fairly risk-averse by nature, but I accept the fact that there will always be risk and I will never have all the answers, nor will I be prepared for every single thing that comes my way.

I also realise the beauty in not preparing for every single little thing. It is often those times of uncertainty or doors that close that open us up to so many other wonderful, new opportunities that we would never know existed otherwise. Even though I cancelled my event because of COVID-19, I can say that it has made some areas of my strategy much more laser-focused than before. As a result of this virus, I am creating some exciting things that I would not be doing if it wasn't for this situation. And as far as my event, I am now working on a virtual version of it until we can all safely be together again.

I define Legendary Leadership as leaning into the temporary discomfort to avoid the permanent discomfort of staying where you are. I started my business on temporary discomfort—perhaps deep discomfort and uncertainty. And I continue to sit with that discomfort, because I am still growing my business and finding my way. But the permanent discomfort of staying in my "comfortable" corporate job was a much heavier weight on me than the temporary discomfort of leaving to do something that would directly help more people than the job I was doing.

When people hear my story, they tell me I am brave or say something kind. My honest response is that I'm not brave or any of those other things. It just had to be done.

Regardless of whether it's business or personal life, when I coach or mentor someone or give advice, I now tell people to get used to discomfort. It's okay to sit with it. Learning to sit with discomfort is important for progress.

Pam Durant, certified wellness and lifestyle medicine coach, founder of DiapointME

Where perfectionism is a fear of scrutiny or essentially being 'outcast' for saying the wrong thing, procrastination triggers your fear centre when you try to do too much too quickly. Change is inherently unsafe for your ancient instinctive brain. Both perfectionism and procrastination stem from this need for safety. The safest place for you is where you are right now. Doing anything that is too big or too exciting runs the risk of not being safe and your instinctive brain will stop you at every turn through procrastination.

The key to beating procrastination? Break down your goal into smaller pieces. It really is as simple (and unsexy) as that, but that's not to say it's easy.

How can you tell if you're attempting something too big? I can tell by taking one look at my to-do list. If I sit down to it and then get straight back up and go do housework, the chances are that my first task needs to be broken down into smaller pieces.

When I was first given this tool, a mentor was telling me to create a list of every single tiny task that went into a video series project I was working on. If you have ever created a video series, you will know there are a *lot* of different tasks that go into getting everything up and running.

I was still working my day job at the time, so my time was pretty limited, and I was asking for some help to plan out what I needed to do to ensure that I got the project finished. (At the time, I had a habit of being a chronic unfinisher too!) My mentor told me to brainstorm all the tiny tasks in a very granular fashion.

Here are just some of the tasks that would appear on such a list now:

- *Storyboard video 1*
- *Storyboard video 2*
- *Storyboard video 3*
- *Video 1 script draft*
- *Video 2 script draft*
- *Video 3 script draft*
- *Video 1 script final*
- *Video 2 script final*
- *Video 3 script final*
- *Video 1 shoot*
- *Video 2 shoot*
- *Video 3 shoot*
- *Video 1 edit*
- *Video 2 edit*
- *Video 3 edit*
- *Video 1 export*
- *Video 2 export*
- *Video 3 export*
- *Video 1 upload*
- *Video 2 upload*
- *Video 3 upload*
- *Video 1 landing page draft*
- *Video 2 landing page draft*
- *Video 3 landing page draft*
- *Video 1 landing page final*
- *Video 2 landing page final*
- *Video 3 landing page final*
- *Automation email 1 draft*
- *Automation email 2 draft*
- *Automation email 3 draft*
- *Automation email 4 draft*
- *Automation email 5 draft*
- *Automation email 1 final*

- *Automation email 2 final*
- *Automation email 3 final*
- *Automation email 4 final*
- *Automation email 5 final*
- *Sales page outline draft*
- *Sales page outline final*
- *Gather testimonials*
- *Create image list*
- *Gather images......*

And so it goes on.

When my mentor suggested that I do this, my response was one of horror. Something like, "But by the time I've written the list, I could have done half of the work!" Her response to me was, "Write the list." Mine? "I'm sure this is a great system, but you see I'm really busy, and by the time I write the list, I could have done half of the work." My mentor's response? "Write the list." I tried again… "I hear that the list is important, but you see I'm special. I have a lot on my plate with work, family and business. It's different for me. By the time I write the list, I could have done half of the work. Surely, it's possible to do the project without wasting time on this list. I know what I need to do." Her final response? "If you don't write the list, hire someone to write it for you."

At that point, I realised I was not getting out of writing the list! I respected my mentor so I got over my 'special' self and I wrote the damn list. It was pages long, but I will tell you… It was the first time in a long time that I knew *exactly* what I needed to do next every time I sat down at my desk, and I had everything I needed in order to do it. There were no excuses to go and put a load of washing on, or head to the post office, or clean the fridge. I just… kept… going… ticking off task after task after task until it was finished. Now I have lists for my lists and I love ticking off the tiny tasks. I mean, who doesn't get a sense of accomplishment from seeing those ticks or lines through the items?

If you are procrastinating, then one of two things is happening. Either you're not motivated by the task because it's not values-aligned, or the chunks you are focusing on are too big.

Remember, change happens when we experience ourselves as successful and competent. Ticking things off your to-do list is a great way of demonstrating your success and competence. Why not give yourself as many opportunities to be successful and competent as you can? Breaking your tasks down does exactly that.

TECHNICOLOUR TOOL: FEAR AUDIT

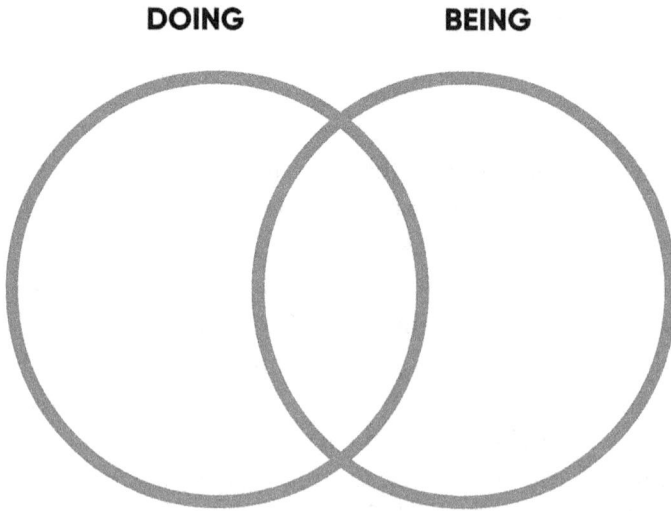

DOING **BEING**

What are you Doing when you are at your best?

How are you Being when you are at your best?

What are you Doing that falls outside of your Zone of Technicolour?

How are you Being when you are performing tasks outside your Zone of Technicolour?

What have you been avoiding or procrastinating over?

Where would it fall in the diagram above?

What have you been hiding from the world because you don't believe it's perfect?

How does it fit with the diagram above?

What are your fears around living a Technicolour Life? Why do you think you have those fears? What does it mean for you and those around you?

What are you saying yes to that stops you living your life 100% as you? What are you choosing and what is the cost of continuing to choose that? What is more important?

What are your fears about being seen?

What are your fears about being you in your work? In your family? In your friend circle?

Summary

Alignment is hard. It can mean making difficult choices and facing fears. I distinctly remember one client who realised that she was in the wrong marriage after doing some of this work. It was so difficult for her to face, but it highlighted to her that she needed to make a change in a way that she could not ignore. The next couple of years were incredibly hard, but she knew she was doing the right thing for the right reasons. Now several years later, I am so happy to be able to tell you that all four members of that family are much, much happier. Both my client and her former husband have remarried to the right partners for them and their children are happy, healthy, well-adjusted and doing great with four parents who love them.

I will say it again. Alignment is hard. That's why most people don't achieve or even seek it. Yes, the result of achieving alignment is ease and flow, but the process of getting there means getting uncomfortable a lot. Now may be the perfect time to review your Commitment To Yourself. If you are Courageous enough to explore what you have learned in this chapter, then you will become more Consistent in your approach to your Technicolour

Life. Consistency is a big part of leadership because it helps people around you to feel safe and secure, either consciously or subconsciously.

And even though this step is Align, you are still gaining more and more Clarity about your own natural tendencies and how to best work with them.

I hope that you have taken some time to really feel into the concepts in this chapter, completed the exercises and answered the journal prompts.

This work is laying a strong foundation for the plans that we are about to put in place for your bold, genuine, authentic Technicolour Life.

CHAPTER THREE

Navigate

"Everything in life has some risk, and what you have to actually learn to do is how to navigate it."

~Reid Hoffman

You have done a lot of the hard work already. You have dug deep into yourself and redefined success on your terms. You have examined the whole blend of your life, not just one aspect of it. You have uncovered your moral compass, or your unique blend of core values; those things that are your non-negotiables in your Technicolour Life. You have begun the process of becoming aware of any limiting beliefs you carry. You have also begun to identify your Zone of Technicolour. You have learned about how fear can impact your results both consciously and subconsciously, and started to change your relationship with procrastination and perfectionism.

Discovery was all about getting to know what success looks like for you.

Aligning was about identifying obstacles and blocks so that you can be aware of when you might be out of alignment in the future.

Now you need a plan!

If you are not used to living in technicolour yet then you need to make a plan that is going to work, a plan that is going to give other people confidence in you as you build your own self-confidence. Since change happens when you experience yourself as successful and competent, you need to create a pathway that will allow you to experience exactly that.

What you focus on e x p a n d s, so your plan will focus on what you want *more* of, rather than what you want *less* of, and doing this consistently. Thinking back to our three keys of Legendary Leadership, the previous chapters had a substantial focus on Clarity and Courage, but planning is where Consistency comes in strongly. And I don't know about you, but I find Consistency the hardest thing to achieve in my life. Even with all the knowledge I have about the benefits of being consistent, I still struggle with it. Having a plan that works and recognising where I need to get some support is what allows me to be more consistent.

In this Navigate chapter, you will create your plan to navigate your way to your bold, authentic, genuine Technicolour Life and become the Legendary Leader you were born to be. Technically, we are all the navigators of our own lives, but how much did you believe that before you picked up this book? Life is certainly an adventure, and making the most of that adventure—whether you like a high-stakes adrenaline-fuelled experience, or a more sedate pace—still requires a bit of planning or thinking ahead of time. Even if the thinking is that you don't want to know the outcome, that is still an outcome.

In this chapter, we will look at ways to create direction in your life so that you can find enough Consistency to live your Technicolour Life. Consistency remains a pillar of Legendary Leadership even if you love spontaneity, because it's easier to be spontaneous when you have the consistency and certainty of a plan or vision. Committing to that vision ensures that there is still plenty of space to have fun along the way.

By the end of this chapter, you will know how to create an environment in which you can be at your best. You'll be able to set goals, visions or dreams as well as have a robust and achievable plan to reach them. And you'll know why you have to do this in a certain way. You'll be equipped to keep going when life throws you inevitable curve balls.

From Following to Leading

Something my clients all have in common is an acute sense of being a fraud or an imposter. While, logically, they can see the evidence of their accomplishments and success, they are always waiting for the other shoe to drop or to be found out. They put their success down to lucky breaks or opportunities, even though they have worked really hard to get where they are, often in the face of barriers such as gender, race, sexuality, background etc.

What drives them to keep pushing ahead—until they come to work with me, that is—is their fear that someone will catch up to them and discover they're not as smart or talented as everyone seems to think they are. When you operate in this manner, it keeps you from your Technicolour Life. It stops you from feeling genuine and authentic, and while you might be taking bold steps, they are not for the right reasons. If this sounds familiar, let's set to work to change this, because until you see yourself for the unique person that you are and know that you don't have to try to be someone else, your Technicolour Life will remain elusive.

You have already seen that the way you process information is entirely different to everyone else and that your particular blend of filters results in your own unique view of the world. You have also seen that you have your own values system, with your own definition of each of those value words, and your own hierarchy or priority system for them.

You are already completely unique.

In order to be 100% you in your own Technicolour Life, a success by your definition, you need to embrace this and recognise that it is valuable. Your unique view of the world is something that allows you to bring something uniquely yours to the table every single time. That something is just as worthy and valuable as anyone else's point of view.

The sense of being an imposter or fraud comes from comparing ourselves unfavourably to others. Just as you have seen time and again in this book, we are conditioned this way. It has to be that way when we are growing up because we need to look to others to learn how to behave, understand what is acceptable and what is not, and figure out how to achieve.

At what point do we stop following and take the lead?

The answer is right now.

Now is the time to take all that you have learned about yourself and take some leadership in your own Technicolour Life.

I love Dove adverts that empower women and was watching one on YouTube recently. It was an experiment that they filmed to help women see themselves as others see them. The producers had brought in a criminal sketch artist to draw the women from their descriptions of themselves. The experiment is shot in a large loft building with just the artist, his easel and pencils and a couch facing the window where the subjects sit for him, one after another. In between the artist and the couch was a sheer curtain so that the artist couldn't see the woman who he was drawing. The artist would ask each woman a number of questions about her facial appearance, then interpret her answers into a sketch. Then each woman would leave.

Later in the day, some new subjects came to the loft. These were people who had volunteered to help out and had been introduced to one of the first group of women earlier in the day. They had been instructed to get to know them a little. The set up was the same with the artist at his easel and the new interviewee on the couch separated by the sheer curtain. The artist asked the same questions, but this time the subject was describing the woman they had met that morning, not themselves. The artist interpreted their answers in a similar fashion.

I'm sure you can see where this is going. The two images of the same woman were startlingly different. Those where the woman was being described by someone else, rather than describing herself, were arguably more beautiful and brighter.

The point is that we don't see ourselves the way that others see us. That doesn't make us a fraud or an imposter. It is just the way it is.

TECHNICOLOUR TOOL: GETTING PERSPECTIVE

If you were to describe yourself physically to someone, what would you say?

If your best friend was to describe you physically to someone, what would they say?

If you were to describe your character to someone, what would you say?

If your best friend was to describe your character to someone, what would they say?

Stop apologising for who you are. Stop wasting time worrying about something that is very unlikely to happen. Stop comparing yourself to others.

Easier said than done, I know. So let's look at how you might reframe imposter syndrome and comparison-itis.

I have used this quote as a beacon for my own imposter syndrome and comparison-itis. Many clients have found it helpful over the years.

"Follow not in the footsteps of the masters.
Seek what they sought."

~Matsuo Basho,
17th century Japanese poet

When I first heard this, it blew my mind. I was just coming out the other side of one of my biggest business failures. I had spent months and countless thousands of dollars relaunching my business after moving from Scotland to New Zealand. I share it here because it's important to see the mistakes as well as the inspiring successes.

When we made the move to New Zealand, I was just two years into my coaching career and I was beginning to find some clients. I wasn't doing life coaching so much as I was helping other service-based business owners get clients—hello, imposter! I was definitely not qualified to be teaching business skills or online marketing to these business owners, but they were seeking me out because I was a couple of steps ahead of them. As such, they really wanted to pay me to help them out. I took it as a sign that I was on the path to becoming a business coach and ran with it. By the time we got on the plane, I was beginning to see a future in the business coaching small service business owners' space.

After getting settled in New Zealand, I turned my attention towards what I was going to do to make an income. My husband had a job, which was fine, and my initial plan was to keep my business going throughout the move. It turns out that I am not in fact WonderWoman. Keeping on top of everything while integrating us as a family in a new home, new country, new everything was unrealistic. After a while, I decided it wouldn't be a bad idea to check out some job opportunities as it might help with getting to know people.

I ended up with two job offers; one that was more related to coaching and helping others; the other an engineering contract. My heart was in the helping role, but the employer had confided in me that I was seriously over-qualified for the job and she didn't know if there was a path to promotion given the size of the organisation. The engineering role was a six-month contract with a daily rate that paid more than a week's salary of the coaching job. My head won out and I went back into engineering.

This meant that I had lots more resources to divert to my business venture and I set to work hiring a designer, a web developer, a list builder and an admin assistant. (Lists were created a little differently back then. I shudder when I think about it now, but that's who I felt I needed to hire at the time.) I poured so much money and time into planning this version of my business, because I had the space to do it at last. I had a great income and there was no pressure to find clients for the business.

As I spent yet another night busily telling my husband about the complicated plans I had for my venture, which involved a year-long curriculum for a business incubator programme idea I had, he turned to me and said, "So are you ever going to actually launch it?"

Ouch! That really stung.

It propelled me into action and I sent 5000 emails inviting people to a teleseminar. (We didn't even have webinars back then.) On the call, I was going to release The Entrepreneur Academy. The day came and I joined the call. There was one other person on it. And that was my admin assistant! Not only that but we got some really angry emails from people who didn't appreciate the invitation to the teleseminar. (We were on the right side of SPAM laws, but only just.)

I was pretty crushed.

There were a lot of things in that experience that I did wrong. The whole case study could be fodder for us to pick apart as far as what not to do as an online coach! However, the main point was that I was following in the footsteps of the masters. I was consuming everything that Ali Brown, one of the most recognised entrepreneur coaches in the world and one of my all-time favourite mentors, put out. I was investing in courses and masterminds and soaking up information like a sponge. I followed all the advice to the letter. Remember, I know how to follow a process and succeed!

The piece that was missing was that I was following blindly, even copying, what my mentors were doing, but I wasn't clear on why they were doing it. If I just did what they told me, I thought I would be successful. *My* reason for doing what I was doing was because *they* were doing it. *Their* reason was much deeper. Their reason was to make an impact, to raise capital to donate to charity, to change the conversation in their industry, to break through glass ceilings. In short, their reason for doing what they were doing was to change the world, whereas I was just using tactics that seemed to work for others.

When you are a Legendary Leader in your life, people are drawn to your authenticity, your sense of being bold, your outlook on life. This means that they are much more likely to listen to what you have to say. Whether that is in a work environment, business, friendships or relationships, it's all the same. People are buying into you. That's why we seek to be genuine and authentic. People can feel when others are not being genuine and authentic. It doesn't feel good.

So even though I was doing all the right things, I didn't feel genuine or authentic, because I felt that I wasn't qualified to do the job I was offering. I wanted to coach professionals and business owners, not be a business coach. There is a very powerful difference between those two. I wasn't clear enough on my deep reason for the tactics I was employing, beyond "because my mentor said so."

By the time I came across Matsuo Basho's quote, it was all beginning to make sense to me. I was focusing on the footsteps, not the bigger vision that would carry me through the tough times. More importantly, it helped me to see that my reasons were different to everyone else's reasons; that my vision kept me in my lane, and that meant that I didn't need to compare myself favourably or unfavourably to anyone else ever again!

Copying or comparing yourself to others is a sure-fire way of keeping you living in the grey. This isn't just true of comparing myself to others in my field of work. It was possibly harder to shift my finely honed skill of being able to compare myself to a room full of people, almost exclusively unfavourably, in what seemed like a split second. For years, I would be able to walk into a party, work event, nightclub or restaurant, and within seconds, I could complete a visual sweep of the room and create a hierarchy of the worth of its occupants. Basically, it was a very simple hierarchy: I was on the bottom and everyone else was above me.

How do you think that affected the way that I showed up in those kinds of environments?

You may see yourself in this behaviour. For some reason, this type of activity—along with feeling like a fraud, perfectionism and taking criticism as a personal attack—are particularly prevalent in successful, ambitious people. How do you feel about competition, personally or professionally? I want you to know that you are not alone; you can still be the best parts of you without the weight of some of this baggage.

It may seem strange to be talking about competition at a stage where we are beginning to develop a plan for the future, but it is actually entirely relevant. How you feel about competition can lead to making the 'wrong' plan for you. If you are focused on your competition for that job, those clients, that role, even that relationship, you may not be coming from an aligned place. Your focus on the competition could be colouring your planning in a way that is not aligned with your values and goals, but instead being influenced by others. Navigating should be about staying on your own course, not reading someone else's map or even having someone else give the directions.

When I first started my business, I really didn't know what I was doing. I mean, really didn't. I was fresh out of coaching school and super excited about my new skills and the benefits they could have for my future clients, but I had no clue about how to find those clients. After having watched the disintegration of my family as my dad followed his business dreams, I had vowed never to put myself under that kind of stress and told myself I would be happy with a safe career and regular pay-cheque, thank you very much.

Here, I was doing exactly what I had promised myself I wouldn't do. So you can be sure I was going to check I was doing it right by getting some education. My local council was running a six-week Start Your Own Business course with an incentive of a £250 grant if you completed it and submitted a business plan. Back in 2006, £250 was a lot of money to me and would cover some basic expenses like business cards, so I was highly motivated to complete the course and claim my prize. Plus, as we know, I am pretty much hardwired to do my best in these circumstances and perform as requested, right?

I was definitely out of my comfort zone as we worked through the basics of business. My overriding memory from that time is of the most uncomfortable part of the whole course: competitive analysis. Who was my competition? What were they offering? What were they charging? What was my Unique Selling Point? It was the most disempowering thing ever. I had gone from being enthused and excited about changing the world to being utterly demoralized and intimidated by others who I perceived to be better than me because they were already doing what I wanted to do.

So what did I do? I started to emulate them. If they had a package, then I had a similar package for less money. Because I was less valuable, right? I had only just qualified. I built a generic life coaching website. You know the one with the pebbles on it? Yup, that was me. And I was constantly aware that I was competing.

Competition (noun)

1. The activity or condition of striving to gain or win something by defeating or establishing superiority over others

Synonyms: rivalry, competitiveness, vying, contesting, opposition, contention, conflict, feuding, battling, fighting, struggling, strife, war

Look at those synonyms!

When you look at the definition of competition it is all about winning and battling and war. There is only one victor, only one prize. Everything about this sets the expectation that what you are embarking on is going to be difficult.

Yet, a funny thing happens when you begin to live your life as 100% you. You realise that you have no competition. No-one can bring exactly what you bring to any particular situation. When you know yourself so well that you can present yourself in a truly authentic and genuine way, you stop competing with others. When you realise that you are no longer battling, struggling or fighting a war to just be seen, you can focus on what's most important to you, which may well be fighting a battle, but perhaps one for injustice, not one inside yourself.

Today, when I am asked who my competitors are by marketers or business coaches, I really, truly struggle to answer.

TECHNICOLOUR ACTION: UNIQUE YOU

It's 100% okay to have role models and people who inspire you, but think about what you are modelling and why. Remember, I thought I was doing all the right things for the right reasons, but it still felt off.

Who do you model yourself on?

What do you admire your role models for?

Are you following in their footsteps or are you seeking what they sought?

What difference would it make to your life to not be in competition with your colleagues or even your family and friends?

Looking back at your values and motivators, what is your reason for doing what you do?

What is your description of success now?

Can you see how unique it is to you?

Creating a Safe Space

When people feel safe, they don't have to be led or driven by their instinctive brain. This frees them up to be able to connect with others on an emotional level, or put their thinking brain to work to be creative or solve problems. Legendary Leaders create safe spaces for themselves and their teams to be at their best so that everyone wins.

If we are going to talk about creating safe spaces, we need to talk about equity. Equity is the pursuit of fairness for all. It is not the same as equality. Equality is about treating people equally, but that does not ensure that everyone can be at their best. Many leaders believe that they are doing a great job by treating everyone equally, but let's look at it from another perspective. In my career, I always thought I was treated fairly, but on reflection, I wasn't. I was paid less than my male counterparts in my job, and I accepted it, because I was a woman. You see, as a woman, I was already behind the start line.

Equity also comes into play in other parts of life. For example, I have two teenage daughters, who are just about to start learning to drive. They are both blonde, slim and white. What do you think are the chances of them getting stopped by the police? Assuming that they are driving well, the risk is pretty slim.

What about my neighbours' sons? They are the same age as my daughters, but they have dark skin. What do you think are the chances of them getting stopped by the police? They are significantly higher.

Let's look at what might happen once they have been stopped. Let's say that they have a small amount of cannabis in the car. An amount that in this fairly liberal country would usually attract a warning for my kids or their friends. What happens to my neighbours' kids? They're more likely to get charged with an offence and end up with a criminal record. What could happen when their kids try to get a job, or apply for university, or for a travel visa now?

In effect, they have been pushed further and further back from the start line because of the perception of the police officer who stopped them.

Now let's look at what would happen if we treated my kids and my neighbours' kids equally. Equality means that they have the same chance of success by applying for jobs, university and working hard, right? Wrong. My neighbours' kids are already behind because of the perception of a police officer based on the colour of their skin.

Equity is the practice of levelling the playing field or putting everyone back on the same starting line. It's not about giving everyone the same; it's about giving everyone what they *need* in order to succeed.

In reality, this does not look like treating everyone the same. It's about getting to know your people (whether that's your clients, colleagues or team) and creating a system that allows them to get what they need and what they want.

One of the less popular but most successful approaches I took with my team members in corporate was to set individual KPIs. I was under pressure to treat all my engineers the same. The same job description, same responsibilities and same KPIs. After all, this was the way it had always been done. If everyone had the same job description, same responsibilities, same KPIs, same bonus structure, surely we were being fair? Nope! I could clearly see that this was not going to work for my team, because I had taken the time to get to know them as individuals, in much the same way as I have been helping you get to know yourself throughout the course of this book.

I knew why they came to work. I knew that some of them were hungry for promotion and success because achievement is what drove them. I knew this because they were competitive mountain bikers and competed in the Coast-to-Coast race, a gruelling event that required the strongest physical and mental characters. I knew that some were providing for young and growing families and they were navigating the increasing responsibilities related to that, as well as not wanting to lose their own identity. I knew that some were driven by money and hung out for their bonuses and pay rises so that they could invest in the stock market and grow their wealth. I knew that some were close to retirement age and were hoping for a fairly stress-free few years before they could pick up their pension. And I knew that some were happy and content in their lower level roles and would rather stay there in a team and a culture that they loved, than search for the next level up in a place that didn't value them as individuals. Knowing all of that meant that treating my team as equals was not going to get the best results for them, for me or for the business.

Initially, my boss was not keen on individual KPIs. After all, we had always done it the same way. Besides, there was a mirror image of my team in the head office and they were sticking with what we had always done. I dug my heels in and thankfully my boss relented. He kept my KPIs and job description the same as those of my counterpart in head office, but gave me free rein to achieve them any way I saw fit.

This was a huge win.

It meant I could begin to adapt roles and responsibilities to individuals. I could not only play to their strengths, but I could also play to their desires. I had the gift of being able to treat people as people and give them what they needed to succeed. I could manage my workload in a way that worked for me and for the team members. The energetic guys who really wanted to be seen as shining could be exactly that and I could push them forward for projects and one-off tasks that raised their profile across the business, while my engineers who were riding out until retirement still had so much to offer in terms of being able to take a balanced and wise approach to their role, as well as being some of the best customer-facing technical staff I have ever witnessed.

At the beginning, there was push-back from the individuals in the team as they saw things as unfair. They thought that some guys were getting an easy ride. However, by taking the time to show them that I had their unique blend of values and motivators at heart, they could see that what I had done was create an environment for everyone to be their best. The result was way less friction in the team. Each person could see their individual path to success. There was more collaboration and a real sense of camaraderie. They would refer to me as their "bullsh*t filter" because they recognised that I kept the politics from head office away from them if they helped me achieve my KPIs.

During the time I was manager, not one of my engineering team left. I had created a place where they could be 100% themselves and succeed.

Today and every day, I create safe spaces for my clients to change, too. It is what you need to do to live your Technicolour Life and to encourage others to do the same.

Before we move onto more traditional goal-planning, take some time to consider what *your* safe space looks like. Hopefully by now you will see that each part of this process is uniquely yours. In delving deep into the Discover and Align chapters, you have brought Clarity to your environment where you can be your best. Knowing this and creating your safe space with your own individual flavour is what will breed the Consistency required to keep going towards your Technicolour Life.

Some of the qualities that contribute to the safe space I create for my clients are:

- *Not sharing their personal information with others.*
- *Not using the information shared in coaching sessions to sell more coaching.*
- *Always, or as far as is practicable, providing the same experience to clients.*
- *Always, or as far as is practicable, having the same backdrop for online clients, the same meeting space for in-person clients, following the same session structure, and outlining pre- and post-session communications.*

Legendary Leaders get this and you can too.

TECHNICOLOUR TOOL: SETTING UP YOUR SAFE SELF SPACE

What type of environment would ensure that you could be at your best?

What does it need to have in a physical sense?

Who do you need to have around you?

What habits or rituals would set you up to be at your best?

You have learned a lot about yourself, so well done for sticking with it. Now we are ready to begin to work towards your Technicolour Life. Let's get an idea of what that looks like.

Describe what a Technicolour Life looks like for you. (Remember, you don't have to get it perfect!)

Everything You Know about Goal-Setting is Wrong

It can be difficult to see the wood from the trees when you are busy being all things to all people. When I trained to be a coach, I learned the principles of outcome thinking and behavioural flexibility. This is something that you are probably already skilled in, especially if you are an immensely flexible chameleon-like creature. It's how you have learned to play within the rules to achieve what you already have. But think about your flexibility working for you in a different way. Instead of being flexible for others' outcomes, why not be really clear on what you want and why you want it?

You have already described what a Technicolour Life looks like for you. Keep this goal close to you and clear as I walk you through a process that actually works for setting and achieving goals.

When I was finishing up my degree and looking for jobs, I would religiously get the Guardian newspaper every Monday because that's when they published the media jobs. One week, there was an advert for a job in London that I was already qualified for, even before I had completed my degree. I applied for the role, carefully following the instructions in the application process, highlighting the areas that were deemed essential skills and speaking to each and every essential and desired requirement on the form.

Shortly after, I was invited to fly down to London from my home in Glasgow for a first interview. It was incredibly exciting. I'll be honest, I can't remember anything much about the interview, but I do remember meeting the team in the studio and making sure that I left a good impression on them. I ensured that they would remember me and I put my finely honed chameleon skills to great use making a strong personal connection with every member of the team in case they had any influence on the outcome.

A couple of weeks passed and I was invited back for a second interview. I flew down again. This time, I remember being in the manager's small, cluttered office and the line of questioning was more around managing logistics. I really wanted this job (and I wanted the validation from being chosen), but I remember being so fearful when I was asked, "When can you start?" I still hadn't finished my degree, so it felt incredibly bold to say that I would like to wait a couple of months so that I could finish studying and relocate countries to take up the position if it was offered to me. I made the most of my short time in London, in case it was the last time I would be there, then headed home and waited.

I got the job! And the organisation was happy to wait for me to complete my degree and move down to London. There had been over 600 applicants for the role, but I had been chosen. That was certainly a highlight, but what I found really interesting was the response from some of my fellow students.

"How did you manage to get that job?"

For me, it had been a process. Put one foot in front of the other until the process is complete. Follow the instructions and just keep going.

There have been a number of times that that approach has served me well in life (like moving from Scotland to New Zealand with my young family in tow). What made it easier was knowing what I was doing and why I was doing it. Getting your first industry job out of university or emigrating from the place you've always lived are pretty big steps to take, so seeing these as processes can be relatively easy. Knowing what you are doing and why you are doing it in your day-to-day life is much harder. If you asked me if I was goal- or process-driven, I would probably instantly say no, but the fact is I am. Getting my first job was just a process. Moving to New Zealand was just a process. Sometimes the bigger achievements can be easier to see when they are broken down logically like that, because otherwise they would be so overwhelming that I would never get started.

In the example above, it was fairly straightforward to identify what I wanted and why I wanted it. I had been on a clearly outlined path and getting that job was the next logical step. What happens when the path isn't so clear or doesn't lead you to the destination you thought it would?

Goal-setting is fundamental to success, but if I am honest, I've had a pretty complicated relationship with it. I can remember countless planning sessions in my corporate engineering career where we set out goals and plans, but I didn't feel personally connected to any of them so I wasn't motivated to contribute. I remember setting goals around health and weight loss over and over again, but without the right knowledge to create a plan that would deliver the results. Oh sure, I wanted it badly enough, but wanting something isn't enough. I remember giving up easily when things didn't come fast enough, like learning to play an instrument. I didn't have a strong enough 'why' to get through the tedious practice and frustration of slow progress. I set goals with my clients all the time, but for a long time there was no consistency in who was going to stay the course and who was going to deviate or give up altogether.

As a coach, this is not great.

Most goal-setting advice does not look at the whole picture. The most ubiquitous is SMART goal-setting. If you haven't come across SMART, it stands for Specific, Measurable, Achievable, Realistic and Time-bound. There is a lot to like about this approach from a logical perspective, but I just don't find it very inspiring. Another piece of goal-setting advice is the Law of Attraction or vision-boarding. This is quite the opposite and essentially encourages us to dream big and that will magnetically pull us towards our vision. It can be more inspiring, but there's no clear plan to get us there. Then there is the advice that you can eat a whole elephant, just one bite at a time. Which is all well and good, but an elephant is a big animal, so am I really going to be able to stay motivated until I finish eating it?

I've spent years exploring what makes a great goal and what doesn't and I uncovered something interesting. Nowhere that I looked did goal-setting address the three brain layers that I introduced you to earlier. Remember the thinking brain (Head), feeling brain (Heart) and instinctive brain (Gut)? These are absolutely critical to goal-setting.

Unconsciously, I developed my art of masterful goal-setting in my adolescence. Now I teach this method to my students and clients so that achievement is simply a process.

Five Steps to Setting Masterful Goals

The key to setting goals that stick is knowing that they must appeal to your Head Brain, Heart Brain and Gut Brain. When you set goals that appeal to

Head Brain, Heart Brain and Gut Brain, you have a plan, you are inspired and motivated, and you are less likely to experience procrastination.

There are five steps you need to take in order to set masterful goals.

1. What do you *really* want?

Most of us don't actually want the goal we are working towards, what we *really* want is the feeling we will have when we have achieved it. What are the feelings that you are trying to reach? For example, you might want to build a business, but what you really want is to feel free. You might want to lose weight, but what you really want is confidence and a sense of achievement and control.

The work that you have done on your values will help you to answer these questions:

What is it that you really want?

What are the feelings you are trying to reach?

Congratulations, you have just completed one of the two steps to align your goal with your Heart Brain.

2. What you are the Reasons Why you want it?

"In order to have what others do not have, we must be prepared to do what others will not do." The second step connected to your Heart Brain is all about coming up with as many reasons as you can about why you want your goal and the feelings that are associated with it. I ask my private clients to come up with 50 Reasons Why! There is good reason for such a high number: we need to get past the surface level reasons to the deeper emotional reasons. These reasons are going to be a fantastic resource for you to come back to when things get harder.

Create a journal entry and call it My 50 Reasons Why.

Start listing all the reasons you are doing what you are doing.

3. How will you know when you have it?

The funny thing about our minds is that they cannot tell the difference between what is real and what's not. We can use this to our advantage by creating a really clear picture for our minds to use as a target. This is a powerful exercise that you started when you defined success for yourself in Chapter One.

Thinking ahead to having what you want, paint a strong, visual picture of what it will look like once you achieve your masterful goal. Do not be tempted to skip this step!

What are you doing?

Where are you?

Who are you with?

How are you being?

Notice the colours, smells, sounds, etc.

What else can you see?

The clearer the picture, the more powerful it is.

4. What are your Stepping Stones?

Now you have a really clear image of where you want to end up and you know where you are today. You have just identified the *gap*. In the same way Indiana Jones had to find a way across the canyon, you too will have to trust in yourself to take the leaps of faith required to make it across yours.

Look at the next six months and break down your journey into six steps. Label each Stepping Stone towards your destination. (Master tip: it may be easier to work backwards from your vision to where you are now.)

What will you call Stepping Stone One: from today to Day 30?

What will you call Stepping Stone Two: from day 31 to Day 60?

What will you call Stepping Stone Three: from Day 61 to Day 90?

What will you call Stepping Stone Four: from Day 91 to Day 120?

What will you call Stepping Stone Five: from Day 121 to Day 150?

What will you call Stepping Stone Six: from Day 151 to Day 180?

5. What are the micro-tasks you need to complete this month?

The single biggest challenge that most people come up against is procrastination, as you saw in Chapter Two. They call themselves lazy, but that's not true. What is most likely happening is that they are trying to take too big a step towards their goal at one time. Maybe this is you.

Heads up! Your Gut Brain will stop you every... single... time. You see, it has one job and it takes its job very seriously. Its job is to keep you safe. Doing anything out of the ordinary is inherently unsafe to your Gut Brain so it ensures that you don't do anything that will threaten your safety.

As such, we need to get a bit sneaky. The way to fly under the radar of the Gut Brain is to break each milestone up into teeny-tiny pieces. It's as simple and as hard as that.

Brainstorm as many tasks as you can that make up Stepping Stone One.

Make each task something that takes less than 15 minutes to complete most of it.

Master tip: When you don't yet know how to do something on your list, make the task to research or learn about it. Don't let a lack of knowledge trip you up.

Now *only* work on Stepping Stone One at this stage!

If you are feeling resistance, it is perfectly natural. In fact, that could be your Gut Brain at work already! My resistance comes in the form of feeling like it is a waste of time to write the list when I have so little time in my schedule already. If you feel that way, lean into the discomfort. This is a process that is singlehandedly responsible for massive productivity in my life.

Summary

The result of this process is that not only do you have a clear map of your plan, but you also have a list of exactly what you need to do to get there, and a whole host of powerful reasons why it is worthwhile when things get tough. I know it can feel like a lot of work. I often feel some resistance from participants in my group program at this stage. However, it is also the investment that will keep on paying off as you take more steps towards living your Technicolour Life. Commitment is the difference between those who succeed in this process, and those who give up because it feels like too much work.

It's perfectly natural to feel like you want to push back at this point. You are realising that to live your life in glorious technicolour and be bold, genuine and authentic takes work and Commitment. There is no deadline though. This is not a one-and-done activity. What you have in your hands is the guidebook to continuous improvement. It is an iterative process, so even if you feel the desire to race through to the answer, the reality is that the answer is in doing the work and giving yourself permission to take the time to do it. (We'll talk more about permission in Chapter Five.)

When you have a Clear plan to help you navigate your goals and vision, it is the scaffolding that helps you to be Consistent, which really is key here. Consistency is something that I strive for too, but I definitely do not have it nailed. I am allowing myself to get better at it slowly. As with all of this work, it takes Courage. In order to have something that others do not have, we have to be willing to do what others are not willing to do.

CHAPTER FOUR

Communicate

"Good leaders must communicate vision clearly, creatively and continually. However the vision doesn't come alive until the leader models it."

~John C. Maxwell

C ommunication is such a vast topic that I could write an entire book it. There is no denying that communication is an essential skill to becoming a Legendary Leader in your life and the lives of others. Here, I have distilled some of the most useful and less-often taught pieces that will help you to communicate with yourself and others better. Since *Dye Your Hair Purple Sooner* is a book all about you, this chapter mostly takes a personal view of communication so that you can be the Legendary Leader who models your vision clearly, courageously and consistently.

The meaning of communication is the response you get.

I often begin my communication workshops with this sentence, writing it on a whiteboard and asking the delegates to tell me what they think it means. What does it mean to you? Here's what it means to me. It doesn't matter what you *meant* to say. Regardless of your intentions, communication is what the other person hears and interprets.

If you are feeling resistance to that sentence, take a moment to question it. Question everything! Maybe you're thinking, "Wait a minute. Isn't communication meant to be a two-way street? I surely can't be held responsible for how someone else interprets what I say. Especially since you have shown us how different we all are." This view is a place of massive opportunity, because most people do believe that they are not 100% responsible for the interpretation of their communication, which means that those who do adopt this approach can quickly become the best communicators in the room.

When you believe that communication is the response you get, you are far more likely to achieve great results from your communication efforts and be understood in the way in which you intended. Becoming a great communicator is a true investment in yourself. There are countless incredibly smart people who have important messages to share. Sadly, many of them are destined to remain unheard because they do not understand some of the key principles of communication.

When I work with leaders of teams, we will often dive deep into their communication with others, but sometimes they are surprised at how much we also look at how they communicate with themselves first. This is deliberate.

You have already seen the power of language in the limiting beliefs section. Everything you have learned there can be applied to your internal and external communication. Feel free to review the language patterns in the limiting beliefs section of the Discover chapter as you move through this Communication chapter.

Silencing Your Inner Critic

Earlier in the book we talked about procrastination and how many of my clients describe their experience of procrastination as them being lazy. I know that they are not lazy, because they simply wouldn't have reached the heights that they have if they were. There is a beauty in taking personal responsibility for your results, but it is not always helpful. I am not suggesting that you blame others for your situation. Far from it. What I am introducing is the concept that we have more than one inner critic.

I alluded to my inner critic in an earlier story about my running away from what I thought others thought of me and the narrative that was running in my head telling me that I was unlovable and would never be a success. This is just one perspective or inner critic voice, but how can there be more than one? I work a lot in self-sabotage and see people who are doing things that don't make sense. On the one hand, they really, really want to achieve something, but they keep getting in their own way and stopping themselves from ever reaching that goal. After working with so many different people over the years, I've realised that there's more than one voice in play, more than a single inner critic. Indeed, there are many!

Have you ever watched the Pixar movie "Inside Out"? It describes what I am sharing here in a fun way. In the movie, there are five key emotions: Anger, Fear, Sadness, Disgust and Joy. Each emotion is a character who plays an equally important part in the story. We all have many parts of us that are all highly important. When we try and do something without acknowledging all of the different aspects of ourselves, that's when we can get into trouble.

Earlier, I talked about my struggle with losing weight and I want to revisit that as an example of what I mean about having multiple inner "characters". (Let's move away from the idea that they are all critics.)

How would each of these five parts respond to my weight loss goal?

Anger

I was angry. I was angry that I had let myself get to a point where I had to make a radical change in order to satisfy my top priority value and lose this weight. I was also angry that my 44-year-old body wouldn't operate the same way that my 24-year-old body used to operate.

Sadness

I was sad. I was grieving for a lifestyle that I had enjoyed. That I had to give up in order to have this goal. There was an element of grief.

Disgust

I was disgusted. Well, I felt ashamed that I knew better. I knew what needed to be done, hell I wrote the book on it! But I hadn't done it, so I felt ashamed of past failures…

Fear

…which led nicely onto fear of failing again.

Joy

But I was also joyful and excited about the prospect of integrity being the value that fitted my need to lose weight. Feeling not only okay in my own skin, but feeling like I could stand up in my integrity and say, "Hey, I wrote the book on this and I'm here in front of you now helping you with the mindset shifts that you need for sustainable weight loss."

Whenever we embark on all-or-nothing thinking, it restricts us from seeing the possibilities from a more positive perspective. One of the most common thinking patterns that I see in my clients and students is all-or-nothing thinking; if it's not this, then it *must* be that.

The reason this type of thinking is so prevalent is because most of us were brought up with conditional statements. Think about how many times your parents or teachers said something like:

> *If you don't tidy your room, then you won't be going on that sleepover.*

> *If you don't eat your vegetables, then you won't be having dessert.*

> *If you don't get your assignment in on time, then you won't pass your assessment.*

It's not such a big leap for us to begin talking to ourselves in the same manner.

> *If I'm not doing what I know I need to do, then I must be lazy.*

> *If I'm not getting that promotion, then I must be failing.*

> *If I'm not spinning all the plates, then I can't be good enough.*

> *If I don't have a perfect relationship, then I must be unlovable.*

If I don't get along with my boss, then they will not respect and promote me.

If I don't help people, then no one will like me.

It doesn't take too much for these narratives to become beliefs. And when they become beliefs, our behaviour changes to line up with them. This absolutely keeps us stuck in a life of feeling grey.

I mentioned back in the Discover chapter that I had gone through a challenge with losing weight, and after I aligned my goal with my values it became easy to lose the weight, but why had I ended up in a position of needing to in the first place? Well, it was through a belief that I had cultivated.

For years, I had struggled with hormones and extreme period pain. I had been through every treatment from traditional medicine and alternative therapies to try to alleviate the symptoms. Eventually, I was referred to an OB/GYN specialist who told me that I had run out of options and the only thing left was to remove my ovaries and give me a hysterectomy. I remember leaving the consultation and sitting in my car and just crying. Surely there was another option? Once I got over the initial shock of the recommendation, I began to think seriously about having the surgery, and to be honest there was one big thing that was holding me back. I believed, as a menopausal woman, I would gain weight.

It was this belief that kept me suffering daily from one symptom or another for over a year before things became untenable and I went in for surgery. Incidentally, in surgery, they discovered that I had been suffering from undiagnosed endometriosis for years.

The change was immediate, especially the pain, which was great. Except for one thing...

I was gaining weight.

The truth was that I wasn't gaining weight because I was now a menopausal woman. I was gaining weight because of the belief that I had been cultivating for years. Let's be honest, if the weight gain was because of my time of life, I wouldn't have been able to lose the weight and keep it off, would I?

The impact of your inner critic can be summed up by one of my favourite quotes:

"Be careful of how you are talking to yourself, because you are listening."

~Lisa M. Hayes

TECHNICOLOUR TOOLS: MEETING YOUR INNER CHARACTERS

What names can you give to some of your inner characters?

How do they show up? (You might like to think of each of your emotions as a different inner voice or character.)

What are each character's all-or-nothing beliefs?

What do you need to say to each character?

Internal Beliefs of Legendary Leaders

When I was very young, maybe four or five, my mum was trying to get me to finish my dinner. There was a piece of tattie scone (the Scottish version of a griddle scone, often served fried, in case you were wondering) left on my plate and she was doing her best to encourage me to finish it. I'm sure she went through all the usual tactics of bribery with treats or ice cream, threats of removal of future treats—I'm sure she would have promised to feed it to the dog if only we had one.

In a moment of brilliance, she decided to appeal to my kind streak and said, "Och, the poor thing is lonely on the plate there all by itself. You should eat it so that it's not lonely anymore."

You would think that would be enough. Not for this stubborn madam. What do you think I did? Eat up? Offer it to my big sister? Plead with my mum to let me leave the table?

Nope.

I cut it in half and told my mum it wouldn't be lonely anymore!

There are *always* alternatives to what you perceive your choices to be. Helping you see your alternatives is what I love to do.

It's so easy to get caught up in all-or-nothing thinking, especially when things seem challenging. "If it's not this, then it *must* be that." But the truth is that there are always other options. Legendary Leaders know this and always find another option.

That's just one belief that Legendary Leaders choose to live their life by. Just as you have been developing your own rules to live by, giving yourself permission to do what you need to do in order to live your Technicolour Life, focusing on what you want more of, and challenging unhelpful beliefs, now you are going to design more statements that assist you to show up the way that you want to.

TECHNICOLOUR ACTION: DESIGNING LEGENDARY BELIEFS

These are my beliefs of Legendary Leaders. Use these or adapt your own:

Everyone is doing the best they can with what they have

Every behaviour comes from a positive intention

People are generally good

The person with the most flexibility wins

People make mistakes but they don't set out to make mistakes

There is no failure only feedback

Most people's limiting beliefs about their capacities keep them from accomplishing more than they do

Unnecessary control is resented

People want to improve

Change happens when we experience ourselves as successful and competent.

You do not need to know why in order to change a situation.

Complex problems do not require complex solutions.

Whether these statements are true or not is irrelevant. By acting as if they are, it keeps me in a space of compassion and curiosity. This means that I can be flexible without compromising my values or principles. I can choose to operate in a fashion that supports my Technicolour Life.

These might not be the best beliefs for your version of Legendary Leadership. If you have learned anything so far in this book about what makes you a Legendary Leader, it is that everything that you do must be true for your unique view of the world.

Remember when I talked about the difference between values and beliefs in the Discover chapter? I told you about some of the unhelpful beliefs that I had created for myself. It was hard but I managed to change them by adopting new beliefs that would support my new goals in living my life, my way. I discovered that while I was chipping away at these deep rooted beliefs that were created in childhood, I could create a scaffold that held me up and changed my path. By adopting the exact same principle that embedded unhelpful beliefs, I realised I could install new, more helpful beliefs.

Affirmations are a powerful tool when it comes to belief change. I'll be honest, I used to be a real sceptic when it came to affirmations. I thought they were wishy-washy at best, and I was terrified of them at worst and it is all because they were never explained to me in a way I could understand.

I was terrified because I was told that I had to look in the mirror and believe what I was saying for me to get any benefit from them. I simply couldn't bring myself to look in the mirror and lie! Which is essentially what I was being asked to do. But that's actually backwards. In order to believe, you must say them, and repeat them over and over.

You see, affirmations are not for your conscious mind. Your conscious mind is the part that you can hear telling you what you should be doing. It's where you keep your to-do lists and where you weigh up pros and cons of decisions you are making.

It's not the same place that beliefs are embedded.

That's your subconscious mind.

Affirmations are for your subconscious mind. They are creating a picture of what you want more of in your life (if you are doing it consciously).

In my story about my being like my dad, I heard that so many times that it ended up in my subconscious. I believed I would be like my dad so deeply that I was making decisions and taking action that was moving me towards that outcome subconsciously, even though logically and consciously I didn't want to go there.

Remember, my definition of self-sabotage is doing things that don't make sense. Beliefs work far deeper than conscious thought, and they will always win over logic. But you can change that.

Whether you are a believer or a sceptic of affirmations, here's what's really going on when you practice them. When you create a list of statements that would be helpful to you living your life in glorious technicolour, you don't have to believe them yet. You just need to give your subconscious mind lots of opportunities to hear and see them. Over time, they become embedded and serve as a map to guide you to that life of being bold, genuine and authentic.

What we focus on expands. When I was learning to ride a motorbike, my instructor, who rode behind me, had a one-way radio where she could talk to me through an earpiece, but I couldn't answer back. She would often say to me, "Eyes up, look where you want to go. Eyes up, look where you want to go." That piece of advice saved my butt more times than I can remember when I was riding, because when you see an obstacle like a pot-hole in the road ahead, where are your eyes drawn? To the pothole, right? And the narrative in my head would be, "I don't want to ride into that pothole. I better avoid the pothole. If I hit that pothole, I could come right off this bike." What was I focusing on the whole time? Of course, it's the pothole. And so, what happens? I ride straight into it! If I was looking where I wanted to go, I would be focusing on the path past the pothole and would smoothly keep on riding.

TECHNICOLOUR TOOL: CREATING LEGENDARY AFFIRMATIONS

When you create statements to use as affirmations and refer back to them often, they become your beliefs. And if you choose the right statements, they will magnetically pull you towards your vision for your Technicolour Life.

What beliefs or fears are limiting you from reaching success?

What statements can you create that will support your bold, genuine, authentic life?

Where can you look at these supporting statements often?

We can load up that inner voice with new mantras to get stuck in your head. And it's really as simple as repetition.

This exercise was an absolute game-changer for me. I credit this simple shift (and the commitment to practicing it) with the transformation of my entire outlook on life.

Committing to really examining how you communicate with yourself is a lifelong practice and one that will set you apart from most others. What I have found in my experience with working with so many clients is that long-term, sustainable success has everything to do with mindset. Your internal communication is constantly shaping your mindset. It is up to you what shape you want it to take, but Legendary Leaders choose to create a positive supportive mindset through the techniques shared in this book.

External Communication and the Compromise Myth

Now let's look at communicating with others. External communication doesn't have to be divisive or provocative. External communication is your opportunity to inspire, to motivate, to really lead in a way that is aligned with your values and who you are. When you adopt the beliefs of Legendary Leaders as well as your own, with a healthy, positive internal mindset and are operating in a values-aligned way, your external communication will naturally follow. Your voice and message will develop over time when you use the Clarity that you have found through the exercises in this book. Your Consistency in your message will grow as you test and tweak it based on the response that you get from others. You just have to tap into your innate Courage to start. We will talk about permission in the Empower chapter next, which will also help as you begin to Communicate to the outside world as the bold, authentic, genuine Legendary Leader that you are.

The one thing that stops many people from communicating in a values-aligned way is fear of conflict. We can't really talk about communication without talking about conflict. With each individual in the world operating from their own truly unique blend of values, beliefs, experiences and goals, there will always be occasions where conflict arises. The great thing about conflict is that it only appears when there is passion about a subject. When people don't care, they don't care! And I see the fact that there has to be care and passion in order for conflict to be present as a very positive thing. Conflict and having a way to move through it with grace is a very necessary tool in your communication toolkit.

Let me introduce you to the Compromise Myth. The Compromise Myth is a fresh look at working with conflict and creating win-win outcomes. It can be helpful to think about two uses for this tool as I walk you through it. Firstly and most obviously, it is a useful approach when brokering resolution between parties. Those parties could be family members, or they could be colleagues or friends. You might be one of them, or you might not. And secondly, it can be helpful to think about how you can use the Compromise Myth with those different parts of *yourself* that we talked about in the Silencing Your Inner Critic section.

It's natural to presume that the way to get two conflicted parties back on the same page is to get them to meet in the middle. There should be some compromise on both sides, right?

Wrong.

When people are in conflict, what they are really doing is defending their values, because it is their values (or the *meaning* that they have placed on the conflict) that are really at risk here. At the beginning of the book, I told you about the eruption that happened in the kitchen between my daughter and my husband. My daughter was defending her need to feel in control of something in her life at a time when everything felt uncertain. My husband was defending his need to also feel control at the same time. They were actually in agreement, but it caused a huge conflict.

When I was working as an engineering manager, one of my engineers was a real high flyer and he was incredibly smart. Let's call him Jason. Sharp as a tack and with a brain that went 100 miles an hour, Jason was a star. However, Jason had little to no tolerance for people who were not as smart as he was.

One particular week, we were helping the business sales team with an enquiry and the customer's location fell into the area that Jason looked after. We needed to help the sales team explain the fact that because the customer was in a rural area that some parts of their operation would need a booster for signal.

I had asked Jason to complete an assessment on the level of service in the customer's location and make a recommendation about what we needed in order to boost signal levels.

Jason wasn't very happy about doing it, because it took his focus away from another project that he was working on that he was enjoying and it was giving him an opportunity to improve on a process that we had been using. Jason's assessment was comprehensive and jam-packed *full* of jargon: HDSPA, 4G, dbM, Cell-Fi, Free Space Path Loss, etc. It had heatmaps and figures that meant *nothing* to anyone outside of our team.

Jason did a great job of the assessment…

….if his audience was another engineer.

Fortunately, Jason had sent his assessment to me before circulating it outside of the engineering team to customer service and sales.

And I sent it straight back to him!

Not only was Jason frustrated about having to take time out from the other project, but he was now even more frustrated because I had sent it back to him to redo.

That kind of thing can be really common and could have had me tearing my hair out, if I hadn't known what was going on. What could be seen as difficult and belligerent behaviour is actually just an indicator of something much deeper.

There are two very different sets of priorities at play in my scenario with Jason.

My Priorities

Perform the analysis in a timely manner

Get a clear explanation of the situation for the customer

Make a number of recommendations based on service vs cost

Jason's Priorities

Rush the job to get back to a preferred project

Make it as easy as possible for him to complete the job quickly

Do what he has always done

Refer back to the success I mentioned earlier in setting individual KPIs for my team members. I took time to understand every team member's specific core values and motivators. By doing this, I also knew what drove them. For Jason, it was finding efficiency in existing processes. This meant creating projects that he thought were a priority and would work on in his own time for the benefit of the team. Another one of Jason's real drivers was to be seen as smart. It's very important to Jason to be seen as the intelligent, motivated individual that he is.

Knowing this, I was able to show him that he would appear smarter to those other teams by working on his communication to make it easy for anyone to understand. When he saw that his complex and convoluted documents and reports weren't actually being read because they were meaningless to the readers, as opposed to being useful, Jason discovered that being useful was more important than being seen as smart. And that actually, when he could distil very complicated information into a language that the other teams could understand and use to make their jobs easier, they began to see Jason as the go-to guy. His profile began to rise across the whole organisation.

Until we can get the conflicted parties to agree on something, there is going to be a challenge in getting them to compromise. So agreement has to come before compromise. That might sound backwards, but we don't need them to agree on the issue at hand. We need to get them to agree on *anything*. Without agreeing on *something*, it is going to be difficult to reach a compromise, because the two parties are adversaries.

As soon as you can get them to agree on *anything*, they become on the same team again. That's not to say that there isn't still work to be done, but by reaching agreement on *something*, your combatants have experienced that they can agree.

Often, this is a shift that you will be able to feel.

Even if you have to get them to agree that the sky is blue and that tomorrow is Thursday, the nature of having agreed on something shifts the energy of the conflict. Now, you can begin to work down layer by layer into the details to figure out a compromise.

Another way to think about this is to imagine our adversaries are on different levels of communication or thinking. It makes sense to want them to meet in the middle, but that's actually really hard for them to do while they are still defending their position of being right. In reality, they are both probably right, but because they are on these different levels of thinking and communicating, they can't see it.

And so we use a process called 'chunking'.

We chunk up to reach agreement on anything. This is very similar to what you have just learned. In chunking up, we are trying to get the benefit of perspective and get our adversaries out of those survival or instinctive layers of thinking. We ask questions and make statements like:

What does this mean?

Let's look at the bigger picture

How does that relate to…?

What are we trying to achieve here?

Who is this for?

What do they really want?

The further up the levels of communication and thinking we go, the more likely we are to find common ground. In this type of questioning, we are moving towards the bigger picture.

In my experience with engineers, it might be that they want the gold standard in equipment, but the senior leader has to balance budgets. The questioning might lead back to the vision and purpose of the company. We can all agree that we want to provide a world-class service that connects our customers. That's the point of agreement. It is intentionally generic.

Then we can begin to chunk back down towards the details of *how* we go about providing a world class service that connects our customers. When chunking down, we ask questions and make statements like:

What specifically...?

Tell me more about...

What is the root cause of all of this?

What needs to happen for...?

In our engineer example, I might ask, "What needs to happen for us to provide a world-class network that connects our customers from an engineering perspective? What also has to happen to provide a world-class network that connects our customers from a customer support perspective, a marketing perspective, a sales perspective, and a human resources perspective?"

By first reaching agreement that each person wants the same goal, it becomes easier to chunk down into the details and reach a well-balanced compromise. This is an approach that you can take with projects too.

Use chunking in both directions to get clarity and understanding:

Start at a high level to define the problem

Chunk down to find project goals and milestones

Chunk up to review and agree

Chunk down to deepen understanding of the problem

Chunk up to identify problems in the overall system

Chunk down to allocate specific tasks

TECHNICOLOUR TOOLS: CHUNKING FOR COMPROMISE

Legendary Leaders are curious in their communication and spend far more time in their interactions listening and asking questions than they do talking.

Where can you see this technique being useful?

When you think about a typical conversation, what percentage of it do you spend talking?

When you think about a typical conversation, what percentage of it do you spend listening?

When you think about a typical conversation, what percentage of it do you spend asking questions?

When you are thinking from the perspective of the Compromise Myth and finding agreement through the maze of conflict, it forces you to listen and ask questions rather than force an answer. This reduces the pressure on you to always be 'right' and it empowers those around you to begin thinking bigger and developing their own solutions to problems, challenges and conflict.

Based on your answers to the questions above, would you like to increase the amount of time you spend listening and asking questions?

How will you begin to do that?

Summary

Clarity and Consistency in your communication come from the Courage to look inside and look first at how you communicate with yourself. It is no surprise that the three pillars to Legendary Leadership are present at every step in this process.

In order to become a great communicator with others, you need to first become a great communicator with yourself. Get to know all the voices that your inner critics use and become curious about their perspective on your life. Remember each one is playing an important role and is actually looking out for you. When you can begin to see that, you have the power to be able to negotiate with your own inner critics and feel supported rather than scrutinised and criticised by yourself.

Create a set of affirmations or belief statements that will support you as you want to be and refer to them often.

And remember that meeting in the middle is not going to get you where you want to go when you experience or come across conflict. Reach agreement before compromising.

CHAPTER FIVE

Empower

*"I want to be the best daughter and wife and friend and person
I can be. And I want to help empower the people around me to
be the best they can be."*

~Chelsea Clinton

Over the course of the previous chapters you have learned, you have discovered and uncovered, you have become curious and you have challenged your beliefs. Congratulations! Some of that work is really hard. Now is the time to set you up to be empowered to go on and take everything you have learned and apply it to your technicolour future so that you can live the rest of your life in the knowledge that you are being 100% you. It's time to empower yourself and others.

Why do we need empowerment?

In 1983, at 10 years old, I was part of a school production. My primary school classmates and I were performing four numbers to represent the seasons and I was in the group assigned autumn and the song "Shine on Harvest Moon". Like everything in school, I wanted to do my best, and I took direction from my teacher well. The autumn group consisted of three 'couples' and we were hamming up our parts as husbands and wives in the skit by smiling and gazing into each other's eyes to sell the piece to our audience.

I loved it. I practiced, sang and acted my heart out on that stage in front of a packed school auditorium and felt proud as punch when we came off stage.

Until… My fellow classmates bullied me mercilessly for doing as my teacher had asked. They made fun of me and teased my 'husband' about me fancying him. I felt mortified.

That was when I realised that doing the right thing didn't always result in getting the right outcome. On the one hand, my teacher and my parents were proud and showered praise on me, but my peers could see through me to my weaknesses and vulnerabilities. And they sure did take advantage of that.

I spent large portions of my early to mid life feeling like I didn't fit in. I can remember countless times when I have felt guilty for plaudits and praise that were offered to me to the point where I refused them, because I did not feel worthy. In some ways, I was waiting for the other shoe to drop like it did in my primary school performance.

Now after almost 15 years of working with people to help them achieve goals, understand and get over their blocks and perform better, I have realised that while my school performance experience may be unique to me, the *feelings* are incredibly common.

Over the past four chapters, you have begun to unpack what makes you *you* and started to question what works in your Technicolour Life, and what you need to release or change to better support you in becoming a Legendary Leader for yourself and others. However, if you don't feel powerful enough to take all of this forward, you may remain right where you are.

One definition of empowerment is "the process of becoming stronger and more confident, especially in controlling one's life and claiming one's rights". This is the perfect description of this whole book. In this final chapter, you will pull together everything you have done so far and start to build confidence in the Technicolour Life you have designed.

This chapter expands on some of the topics you have been introduced to in earlier chapters as well as continuing to tweak your perspective and make stepping into your bold, authentic, genuine Technicolour Life much easier.

Remember, when you are overwhelmed or experiencing stress, your ability to process information can be compromised by up to 80%, so I am all about making things easier.

Permission

Back in 2007, I was early into my coaching career and I was working with a client who had a number of challenges. She was struggling to let go of anger over a relationship breakdown with her ex-partner, had challenges at work, and was often frustrated with others' behaviour. I worked with her for 11 coaching sessions trying hard to hold a mirror up to her so that she could see that at the heart of her challenges was her model of the world and how she was in control of changing that. By session 12, I was ready to give up and refund her. I had one more technique that I wanted to try with her and I walked her through it in that last session.

Midway through the visualisation, she said, "I've got it. I can see it now. I'm done." I was pretty surprised to say the least and so I asked her to explain a little more. She told me that by guiding her through the technique she was able to see that she had never given herself permission to be happy. In that moment, she saw clearly the impact that not allowing herself to be happy had had on her, and how giving herself permission to be happy could change everything going forward. It was such an a-ha moment for her that she finished the session early and set about making the changes that would make her life easier and far more enjoyable going forward.

If you want to live your biggest, boldest Technicolour Life, it is time to look at the ways that we have disempowered ourselves through our beliefs and self-imposed rules so that we can begin to empower ourselves and others to be their best.

When we are living in the grey, we know what's expected of us. The rules are pretty much laid out for us and we know how to achieve or even excel within them. But when we choose to step out of that environment and be 100% ourselves, suddenly the safety net of knowing the rules gets whipped away from under us. Now we have choice, but we also have no distinct playing field because we are no longer playing the game.

This can be a blessing and a curse. It's a blessing because now all we have is choice. Choice to do what we want our way. That choice can also be paralysing, especially if you have been brought up to change your colours like a chameleon in the presence of others. We get a lot from achievement, but in order to achieve we need to set clear boundaries on expectations. Up until now, it's likely that you have looked to others for this external validation. When you remove that, you need to find your guideposts in another way.

You have already seen this in the art of masterful goal-setting portion of this book. Our conscious mind needs structure, but all the structure in the world isn't going to help you if you still won't allow yourself to succeed. We have spent a lot of time discovering where some of the blocks or obstacles to your Technicolour Life may be lurking. Now I want to draw your attention to the idea of permission.

You might remember that I told you earlier in the book that I gave myself permission to *contribute* to my industry, to be one of many experts, not *the* expert. Where did this idea that I had to be *the* expert come from? I honestly don't know, but I can hazard a guess that it was something that I picked up much, much earlier on in life. I doubt that anyone ever taught me that there can be only one expert, but somewhere I picked up a breadcrumb of such a rule and ran with it until it became implicit in my mind.

Remember how we need to filter all that information all of the time. It is likely that the filtering process has led to an internal representation at some point in time. The subconscious belief "there can be only one expert" becomes true for me. That belief or 'rule' that I had been carrying wasn't doing me any harm until I began to develop credibility in my field. Beliefs and rules are very similar. In fact, beliefs and rules are both essentially beliefs. When I talk about rules though, these are beliefs that have often been given to you by others. They are your parents' beliefs, your teachers' beliefs, your spiritual leaders' beliefs. This makes them feel more rigid than those beliefs that you have developed on your own.

DYE YOUR HAIR PURPLE SOONER MOMENT: JB

JB is a client who I worked with for about a year. After a few sessions we uncovered a block around success. JB had grown up in a family that was very humble and valued an honest day's work for an honest day's pay. The impact of being around this narrative when she was so little was that JB had a deep-seated belief that running a success-ful business was sleazy and this led to self-sabotaging behaviours whenever she got close to her definition of success. This might show up as not following up leads or discounting pricing options. It cre-ated guilt for wanting to enjoy having beautiful things in her home.

> The culmination of this narrative, which had been embedded over years of conditioning (albeit coming from a good and loving place), was causing JB to stay small in a life that she craved to look so different.
>
> By uncovering this belief, we were able to understand its origins. We were also able to reconstruct it in a way that made it safe for JB to be successful enough to have what she wanted and not feel sleazy.

My belief that there can only be one expert had no doubt been created in a moment of subconscious filtering based on a number of lenses like values, memories, decisions, and strategies, but it was no longer serving me. In fact, it was causing me to stay small, and not step up to be heard.

This is a common story and one that I see in myself and my clients often. We need to break through the rules that we have created for ourselves in order to live our Technicolour Life and be bold, authentic and genuine. But first we need to identify them.

TECHNICOLOUR TOOLS: KNOW THE RULES TO BREAK THEM

What rules are you currently living by that you need permission to break or change?

Here are some examples from some of my clients over the years:

Success is sleazy

There can be only one expert

It's rude or crass to talk about money

Women aren't as successful as men

Work has to be hard to be worthwhile or valuable

Help shouldn't come with a price-tag

Writing a book is self-indulgent

You may have come up with some of your own already in the beliefs section of this book.

What permission do you need to give yourself to live your Technicolour Life?

Now establish the permission you need to give yourself in order to overcome those beliefs. Here are some examples:

I have permission to be successful

Success means I can help more people

I have permission to contribute

I have permission to talk about money

I have permission to be as successful as anyone else

I have permission to do valuable work with ease

I have permission to be compensated for helping others

I have permission to take the time to write my book

I have permission to fail

Once you have your permission statements, refer to them often. What you focus on expands, so focus on having the permissions you need from an internal viewpoint, rather than the external validation that you have been used to receiving up until now.

Speaking of internal permission, remember that you also get to decide how much weight your emotions carry and how you react. Next, we'll examine how to take back that power too.

Take the Power Back

Have you ever stopped to consider what your emotions actually are or why they have so much power over you? If you've ever felt held hostage by your emotions, then you're going to love this. Clients often tell me that if they could just get on top of their emotions, if they could just *control* their emotions, then they'd be able to take the right next action to achieve their goals. If they weren't such emotional beings, then they'd be able to achieve their goals.

Emotions start off as a physiological response to a stimulus or trigger. They are something that we feel in our body, then we give that feeling a description that is the emotion. We can have different feelings and we equate them to different things.

What happens when we have that physiological response and give it a label? Our brain gets involved and our self-talk starts up.

Let's go through the process using stress as an example:

1. Something happens. There's some sort of stimulus or trigger.
2. We have a physiological response somewhere in our body.
3. And then we say, "I'm really stressed".

What does it feel like when you say "I'm really stressed" or "I'm stressed"?

For me and many of my clients, it's scary. It feels like we're out of control. It feels really panicky, like there's nothing we can do about it. Those symptoms that we looked at earlier are becoming stronger and scarier.

But there is some magic that you can apply to this situation. As soon as you begin to notice your own stress symptoms, instead of saying "I'm so stressed" to yourself, what if you changed it to "I seem to be experiencing stress"? What feels different from "I'm *really* stressed" to "I'm *feeling* stress" or "I'm noticing stress"?

Suddenly, instead of the stress defining you, it is now something that is external to you. In fact, now you have control over the stress instead of it controlling you. Suddenly you have choice.

Simply by changing the way that you describe what is going on to yourself, you can take the power back from your unhelpful emotions. You can stop, identify the root cause of the stress, deregulate your central nervous system and increase your ability to make good decisions for you and those around you.

Language is a really important part of the whole Legendary Leadership process. Be careful with your word choices because they can make a huge difference to your outcomes.

DYE YOUR HAIR PURPLE SOONER MOMENT: MC

Have you ever noticed that the simplest tweaks in language can be incredibly powerful? Something that many of my clients struggle with is the idea of competition. They simply don't thrive in a competitive space, but that doesn't mean that they don't want to strive to become better.

I remember a session with a client, MC. He had the same struggle. He is a gifted achiever who is always willing to do the personal development work required to improve, and takes personal responsibility for his results. But he also struggled with the idea of competition as he never saw himself as the alpha male type of person.

When I reframed the idea of competition with ambition instead, everything fell into place for him. Ambition was a word that he felt really embodied how he felt and his actions could align with it and his values.

It's a simple tweak, but it can make all the difference.

The Benefits of Pre-Mortem

We all know that practice makes perfect. (Not that we need to be perfect, right?) The problem with fear is that we don't get a chance to practice, so we are actually afraid of the unknown. That's where the pre-mortem comes in. A post-mortem tells us what contributed to an outcome. A pre-mortem gives us the opportunity to explore all the possible outcomes before they happen.

Before we look at some powerful questions you can use to explore your pre-mortems for situations that are causing you fear or discomfort, I have a secret to share. Your brain doesn't know the difference between what's real and what's not. It's true, it really doesn't.

Let me show you...

Imagine you are in a bright, sunny kitchen. On the bench there is a beautiful, blue fruit bowl full of perfectly ripe fruit. On the top of the stack of fruit is a bright, yellow lemon with waxy, bumpy skin. You take the lemon and place it carefully onto a chopping board, then you reach for a sharp knife that glints slightly in the sun streaming through the kitchen window.

You bring the knife down through the lemon rind and through the flesh. As you do, the juice from the lemon gently sprays out from the gap the knife has created. You continue to cut the lemon into a bright, glistening wedge.

You pick up the wedge and begin to raise it up towards your mouth noticing the individual sections in the lemon and the drops of juice that are travelling down the sides of the wedge.

You open your mouth and take a bite...

Without being able to see you right now, I am guessing that you are in one of two places; either your mouth is watering at the thought of biting into the fresh lemon, or your face is screwed up at the thought of its sourness.

Either way, where is the lemon?

It's merely a picture in your mind.

Why is this important in your quest towards your Technicolour Life?

Well, it means that you *can* practice scary scenarios before they happen. And your brain will think that you have had the experience already. You can practice and practice and practice. This creates the pathways in the brain that help to make what you are about to do much, much safer. And we already know that if your instinctive brain feels safe, then it's not going to trigger your fight-flight-freeze instinct, which is at the root of most fear.

We're afraid that we won't have the capacity to work through what to do next. And when we are stressed, we are operating at a significantly diminished capacity, so what you fear is far more likely to happen. Couple that with the principle that anything will e x p a n d if we place our focus on it, and we have the recipe for disaster. But using the same principles, we can flip this to work for us rather than against us.

TECHNICOLOUR TOOL: WORST THAT CAN HAPPEN, BEST THAT CAN HAPPEN

In order to really explore the possible outcomes in any situation, ask yourself these four questions.

What will happen if you do?

What will happen if you don't?

What won't happen if you do?

What won't happen if you don't?

Whether you fear failure, humiliation, scrutiny, success or increased visibility, these questions will help you to decide how you would *like* to respond. Then you can run through the scenario in your mind to create a desired outcome and motivation to move towards it.

The truth is that reality usually sits somewhere between the best and the worst. From working through this book, maybe you have realised that there is always space in between. Imperfect action is better than no action at all.

Complex Problems Do Not Require Complex Solutions

There is no denying that life gets complicated and complex at times, but that doesn't always mean that solutions to complex problems also have to be complicated. Often when I am talking to a prospective coaching client, they tell me about their struggle and then they express that they don't know why they can't get over it. They are expecting a painful journey into their past to find the root cause and are surprised (and thrilled!) when I tell them it's not always necessary to understand where a problem originated in order to move past it.

The truth is that we don't need to always understand why we are the way we are, or why a problem is a problem, in order to find a solution and strive towards our goals in an authentic way. Sometimes it's far more preferable to take the simple way. When problems seem complex, that is a sign that we are in too deep and it's time to get a different perspective.

Have you ever tried to solve one of those full-size maze puzzles? They were very common in the gardens of the stately homes I visited in the UK as a child. They were made from exquisitely manicured box hedges at a height that meant you couldn't see over the top. Later in life, we took our children to a maze at a really cool PuzzleWorld in Wanaka, New Zealand that had wooden walls with secret doors.

I know that some people love these mazes and have great fun trying to solve them, but they cause me anxiety! I find it almost impossible to work out where I need to go and what choices I need to make from that restricted perspective. Yet, from the viewpoint just above the maze, it is easy to see how the maze fits together and what twists and turns to take in order to solve the puzzle.

Most problems are the same way.

When things seem to be at their most complex, that's usually an indication that we are too deep inside the problem, and that we need the benefit of perspective to see the solution.

As you're reading this book, you are most likely a problem-solver. That's how you have reached the levels of success that you have already achieved, but are you aware of what you are doing when you are able to solve problems for others? And do you know why what you are doing works? If you're unsure or even just curious, you'll find the next exercise interesting indeed.

The closer you are to your challenges, the harder it is to see how all the component parts fit together. The closer you or your clients and team are to a problem, the harder it is for them to dissociate from their feelings and emotions about the situation so that they can have a clear head and objective approach. Quite simply, the further you get from a problem, the easier the problem is to solve. Often described as taking a 10,000-foot view, when you can zoom out of the problem you are facing, you can see far more clearly and be less emotionally attached to the steps you need to take to reach a great outcome.

Visualising distance from a situation means that your feeling brain and instinctive brain are less attached to the outcome and those responses lessen, allowing your thinking brain to take the lead and work out what's going on and what options are available. Remember, being stressed reduces your ability to process information by up to 80%, the equivalent of operating at four grade levels below your actual education level. When we disconnect your stress responses in your instinctive and feeling brains, it gives you back your entire cognitive ability. Pretty cool, huh?

TECHNICOLOUR TOOL: THE 10,000-FT VIEW

This technique is helpful for getting some objectivity on your challenges. When you have a problem to solve, visualise being above it and having it laid out in front of you. Another technique that may be easier to connect with is to imagine that you are watching the scenario or problem play out on a movie screen.

What can you notice about what is going on?

How are the players interacting with each other?

What can you see now that you couldn't see before?

Play with moving your imaginary seat in the movie theatre. You will be able to see more from the seats at the back of the theatre than the front rows. You can even look at the scene playing out from behind the window in the projection room.

What else can you see?

What is the thread running through this complex problem?

If you pulled that thread, how would it solve the problem?

Summary

"Empowerment is the process of becoming stronger and more confident, especially in controlling one's life and claiming one's rights."

~Lorraine Hamilton

Empowerment cannot be learned, it can only be achieved through doing. In this chapter I have tried to make the doing as easy as possible by reframing the way you might have looked at things to remove any remaining blocks or obstacles to your success.

It is possible, or perhaps even likely, that you have been granted permission for what you have done up until this point, but to go further into your Technicolour Life, you need to grant that permission to yourself.

As you will have seen throughout all the chapters, the language that you use with yourself and others is important, and has a massive impact on how you feel. How you feel determines what you do next, and it is what you do that controls your results.

The approaches in this chapter are what makes the difference between Legendary Leaders and those who are not prepared to dig deep to reach the Clarity and Consistency required to live their boldest life. And it is your Courage to do what others are not prepared to do that will make all the difference.

CHAPTER SIX

When Will I Be Successful?

This is a question I get asked a lot in my line of business. There are plenty of coaches who are more than happy to tell prospective clients that they'll be an overnight success, or making six figures in six weeks, or some other grand promise, but because of my values, I can't and won't do that.

What I will tell you is what I tell everyone else who asks me how long it takes to be successful.

Give yourself two years.

Now, that might sound a bit strange, given that you haven't told me what your goal actually is, but one thing I have found is that there is something a little bit magic about that two year mark.

For a long time I flip-flopped from my career to my business. I was working a big day job in corporate as an engineering leader and working on my coaching business at nights and weekends (and some pretty early mornings too.) I really liked my job to be honest, but my passion still lay with coaching others so that I was a bit closer to the impact that I was making.

When things were going great in my day job, I would daydream of staying in corporate and rising up the ladder. I loved being part of something bigger and having a team around me.

But on the days when the travel meant I was missing my kids, or that I had to go, cap in hand, to ask for time off, or I had to deliver a project that I felt had been compromised a step too far, that's when the fire for my business was ignited again and I would go all-in in that.

The problem with this approach was that I wasn't Committing to either, but working super hard in both.

So I made myself a promise.

I promised myself that I was going to show up every, single day in my business for two years. If, after those two years were up, I wasn't in a place to fully go all-in, then I would walk away from it and accept that I was one of the ones who wasn't destined to be successful. That I truly was 'just like dad.'

I set about it, and I worked hard, I worked smart and went all-in to really challenging some of the fears that were holding me back in my business.

Two years passed and I began to take stock. Was I where I hoped I would be? Not exactly. I wasn't making the same money that I was making in my corporate job yet, but when I looked back to where I had been two years prior compared to where I was, there was no way I was going back.

I had the clarity to really know that what I was destined for was being bold, genuine and authentic, and that meant carving my own path.

Two years gave me time to experiment. It didn't always look like success, but by giving myself two years it meant that any 'failures' were not terminal to my goal. (I put 'failures' in quotes because I really don't believe in failure, only feedback.)

Two years gave me the space to test, tweak, iterate and optimise.

Two years gave me time to gather data.

Two years gave me time to make mistakes and not give up.

Two years gave me time to work with coaches and mentors and not expect any one of them to be the magic bullet.

The two year timeframe is not about waiting two years, it is absolutely about taking action from today, and building something over an identified period of time.

I love the timeframe of two years, but success can be accelerated or be more deeply embedded with a success team around you. That might look like working with someone like me in a group or 1:1 coaching program. It could look like bringing together a mastermind of like-minded individuals to support each other through similar goals. It could look like finding a mentor who has already achieved what you are seeking to achieve and secure their guidance and accountability.

My clients work with me because they want some assurance that they are on the right path, while they build their confidence in finding their own right path. They work with me to accelerate the Discovery process. They work with me to help them gain the Clarity and Consistency, and support them to be Courageous enough, to take each next step as you have outlined by completing the practices in this book.

Success might not look exactly as you design it from here today. Be open to the things that are most important to you—your values—and you can still succeed in creating your Technicolour Life.

Remember you have in your hands right now a great resource to come back to over and over again during your experimental period. This book is not meant as a one-and-done experience, it is a toolbox. Use it.

When you can be really clear in the feelings that you will have once you are living your life 100% authentically, rather than what you will be doing or where you will be doing it from, you have far more opportunity to reach that point and truly be successfully living a Technicolour Life.

DANCEing Towards Becoming a Legendary Leader of your Technicolour Life

Just as I DANCE in the moment with my clients in my programs and 1:1 coaching practice, you can now DANCE towards becoming the Legendary Leader of your own bold, genuine and authentic technicoloured life.

You have **Discovered** what is most important to you. You have defined success in your terms. You have experienced yourself as the truly unique individual that you are and I hope that now you can see why traditional advice and values have not served you until now.

You have begun the process of **Aligning** yourself and your future life with your strengths and values. This is a process that takes time and can be challenging. All I ask is that you commit to practicing and knowing that you are worth it. You have taken the time to create the supports and structures that you need in order to make this a lifelong iterative process (*and there are more supports available if you would like my ongoing help.*)

You are now a **Navigator** with a plan that works! You can see the path from following in the footsteps of others which has served you up until a point, to moving into becoming the Legendary Leader of the rest of your life. And you have a plan to ensure that procrastination has become a thing of the past.

You recognise that **Communication** with yourself first and foremost is of utmost importance before communicating with others. You know how to not only silence your inner critics, but work with them to negotiate a win-win outcome that ensures you feel supported and not isolated by your inner dialogue.

And you have given yourself the necessary permission to **Empower** yourself to be the Legendary Leader of the rest of your Technicolour Life. As you begin to show up in a bold, authentic and genuine way, knowing what you stand for and why, your impact and influence will grow and your legacy will be one that will be lasting.

TECHNICOLOUR ACTION: ONGOING REFLECTION

Over the course of this book I have shared much with you as if you were a client of mine. Now it's time to review and reflect and also look to the future.

What were your three to five favourite insights that you learned?

Where are you currently happy and living your Technicolour Life?

Where are you currently not happy and not living your Technicolour Life?

What would you like to be different in that situation?

What do you need to create going forward in order to move more towards your Technicolour Life?

How do you need to be in order to best support you as you move towards that vision?

What other support do you need?

You now have everything you need to get started on moving out of the shadows and into the sweet spot of your bold, authentic, genuine Technicolour Life.

If you're the kind of reader who has read all the way through but didn't complete a single exercise outside of your head, I see you. You probably learned a few things along the way, or maybe you reinforced what you already knew, but without doing the actual work, how will you effect change in your circumstances? As I said at the beginning of the book, knowing isn't enough. You have to actually do the work.

The system is not set up for you to stand out and be yourself and to keep everything in your head. With all the unravelling that most people need in order to move from where they are to where they can truly say that they are Legendary Leaders of their Technicolour Life, it's hard enough without trying to think about it all. I haven't asked you to take time out of your busy life to complete these exercises and prompts for my own ego or amusement. I have done it because this is what it takes to get into action, and stay in action.

How long are you going to spend thinking about it? Because the longer you spend thinking and not acting, the more time your subconscious mind has to find a way to stop you.

How will you feel in six months or a year's time when you stumble across this book in the corner where you left it to "come back to later"? Wouldn't it be better to be six months or a year towards feeling like you are bold, authentic, genuine and living in glorious technicolour?

For far too long, you have kept yourself hidden while you wore your chameleon suit and helped others live the lives of their dreams.

This is your time. Right now. Today. Will you take it?

EPILOGUE

A couple of years ago we moved house, which meant packing up my office, and of course unpacking it at the other end. When I was going through all my years of paperwork, I stumbled upon an exercise I had completed at my very first coach training way back in 2006. It was a future letter.

In it, I had outlined the most outlandish future I could have imagined. I would be living in a sunny place with a home office where I saw clients. I wouldn't have to have a day job. I would spend my time coaching, writing, consulting and speaking. I would be making more money than I ever had before. More than that, I would be relaxed, happy, content, and fulfilled knowing that what I was doing was making a difference to my family and to the world.

Today looks an awful lot like that crazy picture I painted all those years ago when I had no idea what went into creating a life like that. At that time, we had no designs on emigrating from Scotland.

Confidence, freedom, satisfaction and excitement. Those were the things I hadn't taken into account when I used to think about creating a life by design. When you step into being 100% yourself, unapologetically you (whatever that means for you), it becomes easy to take personal responsibility, to prioritise, to say no (or not right now) and to shed that chameleon skin once and for all.

The work that I have outlined for you in this book helped me create the reality that was only a dream when I first wrote that future letter, but now that future is here, where to next? This is lifelong work and will always evolve and change. If I look back to where I was at the beginning of my coaching career, I cringe! I have learned so much since then. Does that mean my clients were short-changed back then? Of course not! I have evolved just as you are evolving now.

I do have a twinge of sadness, though, when I look back at who I was 20 years ago. I feel sad that it took me so long to figure out that I could choose how I wanted my life to be, then find the tools that would help me do that. I feel sad that I accepted the traditional measures of success as my own, even though many of them didn't fit with who I was. I feel sad for the teenager and young woman so wounded by the actions of others who didn't know how to get past that until she was nearly 30. And I feel sad that I didn't know then what I know now: that my Technicolour Life was mine for the taking.

I also feel a lot of relief, which far outweighs all of that sadness. Relief that I did the work, didn't give up, turned my beliefs on their head, and took the risks to feel in control of my outcomes.

No matter how hard it looks from where you may be right now, I have absolutely no regrets about the work I have done, and it is my privilege to walk alongside others as they walk their journey to becoming the Legendary Leader of their own bold, authentic, genuine Technicolour Life.

Now it's your turn. You have everything you need. The Purple Hair Revolution is a movement you can get behind by taking action **now** towards living your bold, authentic, genuine life, just by being more of **you**!

This is it.

Your opportunity to design your life in ways you've only dared to dream.

What would it look like for you with no restraints?

Because **that** is what's possible for you right now.

Ready?

FURTHER RESOURCES

Become part of a community that embraces progress and imperfect action! I'd love to hear your success stories and be there to help you further. Join me at www.lorrainehamilton.net/purple-resources for more updates, bonuses and opportunities to work with me and let's start your Purple Hair Revolution!

MY DEEP AND SINCERE THANKS GOES TO

Marc, Eilidh and Ciorstiadh for putting up with me constantly putting myself into uncomfortable situations.

My Mum for consistently calling me a writer since I was 6 years old, even though it is an identity I am still coming to terms with.

Nicola for looking after Mum and also making sure that everything in my business that needs to be done, gets done. And for being my big sister!

My amazing editor Kris Emery for your patience, expertise, words, encouragement, support and absolute word nerdiness.

Monica Ferguson for suggesting the book title in our podcast interview not knowing that it would be the start of something.

Zac de Silva for being flexible and letting me go off track so that I could come back on track.

Alison Nash for early feedback and encouragement.

The Contributors of stories Karley, Sandy, Caroline, Anna, Sarah-Jayne and Pam. Your stories make this book all the richer.

My friends in life and business, Barbara, Bianca, Amanda and Andrea.

And to all my Purple Hair Revolutionaries—THANK YOU.